RESTORE

A Guide for Truth and Reconciliation Through Traumatic Experiences

By Isa Farrington-Nichols

Inspired by the book
Genesis: The Bullet was Meant for Me,
D.C. Sniper Story Untold

Copyright © 2022 by Isa Farrington-Nichols
Published in the United States by:

Send inquiries to:

JIREH-SHALOM FOUNDATION
www.jireh-shalom.org

Cover Design: Rebecca Pau
Photography: BNW Inc

All rights reserved. No part of this book shall be reproduced, stored in a retrieval system, or transmitted by any means – electronic, mechanical, photocopying, recording, or otherwise copied for public or private use – other than for "fair use" as brief quotations embodied in articles and reviews – without prior written permission of the publisher.

The opinions set forth herein are those of the author and do not necessarily express the views of the publisher or any affiliate.

Farrington-Nichols, Isa

RESTORE

A Guide for Truth and Reconciliation Through Traumatic Experiences

ISBN: 979-8-9854133-0-4

All scripture quotations and references, unless otherwise indicated, are taken from the King James Version of the Bible

This Book is Dedicated To:

SURVIVORS

ACKNOWLEDGEMENTS

Our Father who art in Heaven, hallowed be thy name. Thy Kingdom come, Thy will be done on Earth as it is in Heaven... Father bless the hearers of these words. Bless those that read these pages. LORD, allow your love to conquer and RESTORE. Father, I thank you for the many people that you have sent to me. The many people whom you knew I would need in my life. I thank you for having someone there to help me bear the heavy loads. In my darkest, loneliest hour you placed someone there. Thank you for your love that destroys the yokes of bondage, abandonment, resentment, and pain. Thank you for your son Jesus, an unconditional love that set free and delivered me from the darkest of seasons. Your love lifted me! I dedicate *RESTORE* to my entire family: my two mothers Louise Farrington (deceased), Willie Jean Dangerfield Nichols (deceased), my father James Farrington (deceased), my brothers Joseph (Jacqueline) and Rockwell (Debbie), my sisters Sheila and Lynnell (deceased). I dedicate this book to my two daughters Tasherra Louise, Tamara Jean, my granddaughters Aleera Leah and Tameera Marie, Akeera Lynnell, Terrah Marie. Finally, I dedicate this book to my Apostolic parents, Apostles Stan and Renee Taylor.

GOD BLESSED and RESTORED!

AUTHOR'S NOTE

This is a work of nonfiction.
Conversations have been reconstructed
to the best of my recollection.
This is my personal story and how I experienced it.
I pray that my truth and my experiences support you in
some way on your journey to truth and reconciliation.

TABLE OF CONTENTS

Foreword 1

Introduction 4

CHAPTER 1:   From Then to There to Here 11

CHAPTER 2:   Genesis: Revelation by Revelation 19

CHAPTER 3:   Let There Be Light! 98

CHAPTER 4:   Trauma Intensified 159

CHAPTER 5:   The Beginning of Justice is Near 176

CHAPTER 6:   Greater is Coming 198

CHAPTER 7:   Truth + Reconciliation = Restoration + Redemption 203

CHAPTER 8:   Power + Love = A Sound Mind 216

CHAPTER 9:   In The Beginning, God Created. Period! 224

CHAPTER 10: Re-Membering Me – Dismemberment 230

CHAPTER 11: The Truth Is. A Personal Life Reconciliation Statement 241

CHAPTER 12: Establish Your Purpose with Value 247

CHAPTER 13: EXODUS – It's time to move on! 251

CHAPTER 14: RESTORED – The Life You Deserve Now 255

Restore 261

About Isa Farrington-Nichols 263

FOREWORD

I first spoke with Isa in the summer of 2019. Lee Boyd Malvo's case was pending before the United State Supreme Court -- not to revisit the question of his guilt or innocence, or because he was eligible for release, but to resolve a question about whether some individuals sentenced to life without parole for crimes committed as children, as he was, were constitutionally required to have their sentences *reviewed*. As an advocate working to end the United States' practice of sentencing children to life without parole, this was the last case I, or anyone involved in our reform efforts, wanted to see at the Court. It was literally the worst possible case for the Court to consider, given the nature of Malvo's crimes and the impact they had on the DC region, including on members of the Court who were living in the area when he was on the loose in 2002, haunting communities with a killing spree, as the notorious "DC sniper."

Malvo's crimes also were not representative of those committed by the vast majority of the individuals who would be impacted by his case at the Court. In fact, 25% of the people sentenced to life without parole for crimes committed as children were convicted of felony murder. That means they were not the primary perpetrators of their crimes or did not intend to harm their victims. Like Malvo, a majority of those sentenced to life without parole as children are people of color and were victims of abuse and trauma in their childhoods. Still, all of that would get lost given the notoriety of Malvo and his crimes.

Knowing that this case would, in large part, be battled in the court of public opinion, it was important for us to get in touch with survivors of Malvo's crimes, with a focus on those who might be supportive of our efforts to ensure *no* child was sentenced to life in prison without any possibility of parole. My outreach was an effort to a) tell them what this case was actually about, since it had been inaccurately reported as an opportunity for Malvo to be released from prison; b) offer them an opportunity to have their views included in an amicus brief being filed in support of Malvo's right to resentencing; and c) ask whether they'd be willing to speak with the media about their experience and perspective on the case.

I never take this outreach to survivors lightly. I realize that the reason for my calls, and the focus of our conversations, is triggering, bringing up memories and emotions surrounding what is likely the most traumatic experiences of their lives. Therefore, my outreach comes with great responsibility, compassion, and love, rooted in my sincere hope that the connection I am making will ultimately offer a path to healing.

It is in this context that I had the extraordinary privilege to meet Isa. The first time I called her, we spoke for over an hour. She blew me away with her genuine curiosity, courage, and compassion. Isa's deep faith in God was apparent, and clearly driving her journey toward restoration and healing from the horrific, senseless murder of her dear niece, Keenya. That journey is described in the pages ahead, and has been the anchor of our relationship ever since. It is what brought Isa to DC in October 2019 along with other survivors of Malvo's crimes to meet with

RESTORE

people condemned to die in prison as children who have been freed, and to witness firsthand the oral arguments in *Malvo* at the Supreme Court. It is what brought her to Montgomery, Alabama the following month to visit the Legacy Museum and National Memorial for Peace and Justice, as part of a national convening focused on ending the United States' practice of sentencing children to life in prison without parole. Isa has shared with me that these experiences have brought her a sense of healing and peace. They have also led to a lasting friendship between us, for which I am most grateful.

Isa's deep commitment to restorative justice, compassion for *all* of God's children, and her own pursuit toward healing are awe-inspiring. Her courage to share it with us, including in the words that follow, in an effort to bring restoration not just to herself but to us all, is a truly powerful gift.

--Jody Kent Lavy is the co-executive director of the Campaign for the Fair Sentencing of Youth, and wrote this in her personal capacity

INTRODUCTION

There I was. Seven years after my niece was the first to be murdered by two of the most dangerous, and notorious African American serial killers known by our nation. I stood in a chamber room crowded with the family members whose lives each changed. The D.C. Snipers, John Muhammad, and Lee Boyd Malvo scarred each individual who stood there that day in our own particular way. Yet, we all shared a mutual pain that intersected us at different times and different places.

They saw and knew this man to be a monster. All I could see was John. The man, before the monster, would look at his wife, Mildred, and smile at her with affection. Looking through the protective window as the final moments of his life were upon him, I was seeing John as a father, playing with his three children, Lil John, Salena, and Taalibah. I saw before me the John who lovingly listened to my elderly father and shared stories about business and family. I was seeing John, the one with the apron on, frying cod fish. John was a well-respected businessman. I just could not figure out how I got to this space, in this prison viewing room, with my narrative of trauma. My head was pounding as all the pieces of thoughts scattered around in my head trying to create a picture of reason. I was standing against a wall in front of a large, glass window in the Virginia Greensville Prison's viewing chamber. We were waiting

RESTORE

for John Allen Muhammad's, this man I no longer recognized from days past, to be executed.

Muhammad was tried and condemned to death for the murder of Dean H. Meyers, 53. He was gunned down at a gas station in Manassas, Virginia, on October 9, 2002. My very own niece was brutally killed on February 16, 2002, just eight months earlier. John had sent Lee Malvo to the front door looking for me. His gun and bullet intended for my head. Yet when we arrived back home that day, it was my beloved niece, Keenya Cook, who we found lying lifeless at the door. Now here I am seeing John's lifeless body laid out on the slab in front of me. Would this bring me any closure? Would it bring back anyone that had succumbed to this deadly reign of horrible murders? What happened to John that would lead him down this path? People stood around to watch him take his final breath, to die there while we watched, hoping somehow it would answer our questions and resolve all the pain we felt when he took away our sense of stability and security. I was looking through the glass window at a black man I once knew and cared about, a man who became a spectacle for me, and everyone else there, waiting for vindication.

While leaning against the wall I heard voices on the other side. I could hear someone say,

"Stay here. Turn around." I could hear chains scraping against the floor. I heard someone say once more, "Turn around." And then they asked him, "Are you ready?" To which I heard the reply, "Yes, sir." It was John's voice. I recognized it. I heard a heavy door open, and immediately John Allen Muhammad stepped foot into Virginia's death chamber. Within seconds he was laying on a gurney, tapping his left foot, and his arms spread wide in vulnerability and surrender. I had not seen John since the day I testified in his sentencing trial in a Virginia courtroom. Suddenly a curtain closed in front of us so that they could put intravenous needles into John's arm. The curtain opened, and I saw a needle dug into each arm. "Mr. Muhammad, do you have any last words?" the Warden asked John. John had probably said everything he ever wanted to before he got here. It was in the threats that plagued his wife Mildred. It was in the way he would call my home when looking for her. He was done speaking in this lifetime.

The mastermind behind the Washington-area sniper attacks, the man behind at least 10 Washington DC murders in 2002 was calm and defiant until the end. He refused to utter any final words, perhaps without any regrets. He said nothing about Keenya, nothing about all these families watching for some sort of justice to occur. He said nothing. In what could have been a conversation that saved lives, a conversation of mental health, child abuse, domestic violence, or maybe even marital counseling, perhaps all of these lives could have been spared. After the first of the three lethal cocktails were administered, John blinked repeatedly and took about seven deep breaths. Within a minute, he was motionless. John Muhammad died by lethal injection at 9:11 p.m. Tuesday, November 10, 2011. It was under our watch that he died. It was us, who came from Tacoma, Washington, Arizona, Alabama, Louisiana, Virginia, and Washington, D.C. to watch behind thick glass. The same way he would watch his rampage from afar.

What may have restored justice, did not necessarily restore me. The trauma of the situation remained. From struggling with loss, the need for closure, and yet trying to hold together a family, a career, a smile, the trauma entrenches itself deep within

RESTORE

us, and its manifestations can begin to surface over time, especially if they are not addressed proactively and with the necessary support or resources. Everything that had happened did not finish taking its toll when John was dead. It was just the beginning. Life-changing experiences define the lives we live, and we do have power in how experiences imprint themselves upon our character. Experiences can be good, pleasurable, bad, and undesirable. Let's face it: challenges are going to visit our door. Illnesses and critical health challenges are going to visit our door. Unemployment is going to visit our door. Mortgage payments, rent, evictions, or foreclosure are going to visit our door. A relationship struggle that may lead to insecurity, unfaithfulness, separation, or divorce is going to visit our door. Crime is going to visit our door. Death of those we love so dearly is going to visit our door. John Muhammad visited my door and it affected every part of my life. Do we stand in the doorway and stare at trauma in wonderment? Do we refuse to acknowledge its presence? Do we let it in and accommodate it, so it never leaves? What does a person do when the monstrous traumas come knocking? We spend our lives in search of balance when trauma strikes. When lives experience trauma, lives are never the same. Trauma can put you in an emotional coma rendering hopelessness, depression, irritation, and agitation. Trauma is a Technical Knock Out, a T.K.O. When you get pummeled, the biggest and most difficult challenge is to get back up again with strength and a clear vision in mind. Trauma leaves us dazed and incoherent. You may hear your subconscious conjuring up voices, shouting, "Get up!" You keep trying to get up, but it is not easy balancing between the physical implications and the mental. It is a struggle, but it should be pursued with determination and faith. You must get up, and you can get up! If you stay down, it is there you will be defeated.

The events that changed my life forever are narrated in *Genesis; The Bullet was Meant for Me, D.C. Sniper Story Untold* and into it, I now enter the season of restoration. Everyone can be impacted by the same source of trauma, but each person's narrative is changed in its way, unique from the reactions of others. In that chamber room, I know that I was not the only one who walked out still mourning while others may have felt relief. Some may not have been able to really watch and only hear the voices, whereas others could have been glued to the glass. My story is mine. Yet however trauma sinks into our lives, and however different the implications are, there is a path to restoration. And that path is recognition of the diversity and the need to share these narratives for individual and collective healing and empowerment.

He that hath an ear, let him hear what the Spirit saith unto the churches; To him that overcometh will I give to eat of the hidden manna and will give him a white stone and in the stone, a new name is written, which no man knoweth saving he that receiveth it.
– Revelation 2:17

RESTORE is a book of manna for your exodus. Your exodus is the process of movement from the unbalance trauma brings and into the balance of truth, which reconciles through any kind of trauma. Through a very personal lens, you and I will begin to experience change and transition, in a journey through hardship and restoration of my life enhanced by the strength I have gained. We each have the potential that GOD, the Highest HIMSELF, purposed you to be at. You have a destination to get to. We can make it together.

RESTORE

Oh, daughter, You are so dear to ME.

For I have heard your plea; El, *Shaddai*, the Almighty.

I have listened to you now listen to ME. For I am calling you into your destiny!

I have a call on your life; yes indeed, it has been there since you were in the womb you see. I have a call on your life everything is okay. Fear not, for I am with you always.

Not just a wife, mother, daughter, sister, friend; I have created you to be a woman of GOD. It is time to begin. Abide in ME as I abide in you. I will lead you through. I will continue to BLESS you exceedingly, abundantly indeed, for these things I promised, so continue to obey ME! Look to the hills from whence cometh your help, there you will always find ME.

It is not my desire to let the locust and the canker worm steal your joy for I am *El Roi* the God who sees, the responder to needs. Sow a seed if you do not believe, I will pour you out a blessing you will not have room enough to receive.

Oh daughter I hear your plea, praying for wisdom in what looks like a catastrophe. Do not try to change him, leave him to ME. I am the only one that can heal, deliver, and set free. You are the mother of a child or more, a blessed one indeed. Let them see how fearfully and wonderfully I made thee.

Oh, daughter of Zion, you are safe with ME. For I dwell in a secret place in the Most High. I am refuge and a fortress put your trust in ME. I come to give you, life, and life more abundantly. It is My love for you that I talk to you this way. You were bought with a price. It has already been paid.

ISA FARRINGTON-NICHOLS

It was for love I gave My blood.

It was through MY BLOOD that you are SAVED AND LOVED!

By Apostle Isa Farrington Nichols

CHAPTER 1

From Then to There to Here

*"We can't become what we need to
be by remaining what we are."*
~ Oprah Winfrey

Let's be clear. I am not a part of the DC Sniper story. I am eight months before it. I was not randomly assigned a bullet like the other victims of John Allen and Lee Boyd. It was premeditated. It was planned. It was personal. A 16-year boy was sent specifically to my house to kill me for helping my friend, John's wife, find her children that he'd kidnapped. It was somehow my fault and I was going to get what was coming to me. When Lee came to my house though, he didn't find me. Who he found was a precious young woman. This precious jewel was my niece. Although he didn't physically see me on that day, he followed through with orders to kill me. He didn't find me, but through her death, a part of me died. He stole her life and almost made good on stealing the rest of mine. Surviving John Muhammad and Lee Malvo's malicious attack and murder on my niece Keenya drove me to a spiritual coma. My heart was shattered and eventually broken into a million pieces. That sounds cliche but I could see the pieces of me scattered across the floor of my mind. This tragedy destroyed any kind of human relationships I had and led me into a deep mistrust of everyone I knew. After all, I knew John, and yet he did this horrific thing to me and my family. I was a daughter, wife, mother, sister, aunt, and I had no trust for any of them. I knew the journey to healing my heart, mind, and soul was going to be a crooked pathway, difficult and hurtful in many ways. At the time, I didn't know how I was going to come back to myself.

For much of my life, I had been very on the fence about capital punishment. I relied on the justice system to make the decision based on evidence and testimony. I was a committed advocate of *"Do the crime, do the time"* as well as being convicted to the full extent of the law if that was what the judge ordered. However, when I came face to face with an injustice myself, things changed. When John Muhammad was executed, I did not feel better. It was more death and that day, I got off the fence. I knew John as a father. I knew John as a husband. I knew John as a businessman. I knew John as a friend before he was a murderer. My lens was different from the other people in the room who did not know John at all. To them, he was a monster without a soul. To me, I believed he was also a monster without a soul, but the way I saw it was that he had disconnected from Love. The man I once knew, was no longer in the room laying on this gurney being lethally injected. As I reminisce about it now, he was laying on the gurney like a cross. His arms were outstretched and his ankles were tied down. The warden asked John if he had any last things to say to those watching from behind in the glass, and he said nothing. After he was executed and everyone around me was excited and relieved, I was not. I felt lost. I wondered how this man got here to this place. I thought about how his life growing up as a child and the trauma he experienced then and PTSD he experienced in the military. I wasn't supposed to feel this way. I should have been rejoicing like the others, but I couldn't. It was sad. I was hurt. I was confused. Where do I go from here?

It wasn't overnight or even over a few months. Years went by and I was still grieving, still riddled with guilt, still angry, still mad as hell for what happened to my niece, and knowing that I was the intended target. John had been executed and Lee was convicted as an adult and serving multiple life sentences. Yet, here I was, feeling like I had been convicted. I truly felt like the walking dead. I was here, but I wasn't here. I was present in the world but some days, I was in outer space. The day that this horrific tragedy was indelibly stained on my heart and for many years on my mind. It consumed me to the point of depression and anxiety. Justice, as society would have it, had been served, yet I was still suffering. I was not well in my body, mind, or spirit no matter how I tried to soothe my heart by reminding myself that indeed, "justice had been served." It hadn't though. John was dead, yes, but I was still here suffering. Lee was still here locked up in prison and suffering also, at least that's what I imagined. In my mind, he was living with the guilt of killing all those innocent people and I was suffering from the guilt of survivor's remorse. The bullet was meant for me, not my niece and there is nothing that I could do about that. What I could do something about was taking responsibility for my healing. I needed to do this so that I could be safe and supportive to myself, my children, and in the world. The traumatic experience that I survived forced me to see what is important in my life. It forced me to see ahead of me. It was like looking through the windshield of a car. Not only could I see my future, but it also forced me to examine the truths of past pain. This raw, gut-wrenching truth-telling led me to reconcile myself back to myself. Reconciliation entails honesty, acknowledgment of the painful experience, and letting go of a lot of anger and resentment. This process took me years. On my healing journey, I got a revelation. It was a revelation that at some point I denied was happening. I started to feel sorry for Lee. There was no way I should be. He murdered people. People he didn't even know. Then I started having visions of this 16-year-old misguided boy sitting behind bars. Why though? This is exactly where he should be. Behind bars, rotting away and paying for what he did. This was what my intellect was saying. The conflict came because my heart was saying something different altogether. Yes, I do believe that Lee should be incarcerated. However, how he and many young people like him are serving time didn't sit well with me. What else didn't sit well was all the families left behind? How do we cope? How do we manage? Then what about the communities that had to endure the pain and scars and memories of terror. How does their trauma be healed?

Those were the questions my soul was left to ponder and it was the vehicle that led me to embrace the path of restorative justice. At first, I didn't even know what that was or even had the language to call what I was feeling. I just knew from my own experience that I wasn't ok. I knew the people around me weren't ok, and I knew the country had been shaken to its core with three weeks of mad terror from John and Lee. The remnants were there. The emotional effects of murder were lingering. When I finally discovered a name for what I was feeling it was this powerful movement of Restorative Justice. This movement was the answer to my prayer on how I could heal myself and do my part in healing the community. I say it was prayer because it asks two questions. What harm has been done and how can the harm be repaired? I already knew that the perpetrator simply going to jail or being executed wasn't enough. It didn't help me to heal. It was just a Band-Aid for the wound. For me to move forward successfully, it would take true forgiveness, and let's keep it real, forgiveness can be quite challenging for an unforgivable act. I am proud to say that today, I have forgiven and I've been doing the work to be restored and offer restoration through the Restorative Justice Movement. The ultimate vision for my community healing work is that Restorative Justice will create safer communities and save tax dollars that result in greater survivor satisfaction, a reduction of repeat criminal offenses, and a release of proven rehabilitated men and women back into society. I am doing my part by cultivating a legacy for my niece Keenya, the beautiful soul that started it all. In 2004, two years after her untimely death, I was asked to incorporate the Maxine Mimms Academies, a 501(c)3 nonprofit whose mission and vision are to provide educational and family services to suspended, expelled, and student dropouts to support them in returning to public school. The Academy has three components-- Intake, Academic Immersion, and Family Support Services. In 2010, I became its Executive Director innovating and creating strategies to reach our young people before they join, on some level, the path of Lee and all the young boys and girls whose stories resemble his. Today the Maxine Mimms Academies' model is the demonstration project which led to the passing of State HB 1418 which mandated every school

ISA FARRINGTON-NICHOLS

district in the state of Washington to have Re-engagement Centers for expelled students and dropouts to receive public education until they're 21 years old. Its impact has reduced the school to prison pipeline in the state of Washington, increasing high school graduation rates statewide. When I say "stories," I am referring to the narrative that has played out in a child's life that shapes him or her into the person they are. Many of our children's stories are filled with abuse of all kinds, homelessness, educational achievement gaps, and a sense of being unloved, unwanted, abandoned and rejected. It makes them "at-risk" and susceptible to being manipulated and led into a world of confusion, chaos, and on the far end of catastrophe. The Restorative Justice Movement seeks to intervene and provide hope to these children, our children before self-destruction gets out of control and too far gone. It stings me to say that if there was someone, some agency that could have intervened on Lee's behalf, his life may have ended differently. Just maybe. The possibility is undeniable.

Since 2006 I've worked in the nonprofit arena in some form or fashion advocating for youth and their families. This has helped them as well as helped me to continue turning my pain into power. Through that work, in 2012, I was led to form the Jireh-Shalom Foundation, which is committed to the domestic and economic empowerment of children and their families. My purpose is to advocate for people whom the system has failed -- like Lee Malvo himself, family members, and survivors of crimes. We do not believe that extreme and unusual punishments are fitting for young people. We believe in truth-telling to reconcile traumatic experiences. We believe in holistic healing and self-care. Jireh-Shalom creates a community for those who have lost loved ones to, or have survived violence committed by youth. Currently, Maxine Mimms Academies (MMA) and Jireh-Shalom Foundation (JSF) are conjoined as consulting agencies training others to duplicate the award-winning model.

As I write this compelling memoir of my journey, the world lost a supreme champion of civil rights, Supreme Court Justice, Ruth Bader Ginsburg, and I am grateful to have both been in her presence and apart of creating a meaningful history. Entering into October 2019, I prepared an Amicus Brief for Baker McKenzie LLP for the Supreme Court of The United States (SCOTUS) in the Lee Malvo (Petitioner) vs the State of Virginia. In May 2020, I prepared an Amicus Brief for Baker McKenzie LLP for (SCOTUS) in the Brett Jones (Petitioner) vs the State of Mississippi. Amici are the victims of crime; we have lost loved ones or who themselves have been victims of crimes committed by children. My voice in both of these cases was submitted before the court to show the important diversity of viewpoints held by victims of families who have experienced the devastating loss of a loved one to youth violence. In both these cases, my Amici embraced the rule that life without parole is an unconstitutional penalty for youth offenders. I remember walking into the courtroom waiting with my heart rapidly beating and my mind asking, *"How did I get here?"* How did my journey lead up to this exact moment that my Amicus was in the hands and view of all nine of the Supreme Justices? This feeling left me euphoric even now. More importantly, the three women Supreme Justices, Ruth Bader Ginsburg, along with Sonia Sotomayor and Elena Kagan, were the ultimate prestige for me. When the court was asked to stand as the nine Supreme Justices entered the courtroom, I looked at Supreme Justice Ruth Bader

ISA FARRINGTON-NICHOLS

Ginsburg wearing her black robe with her famous white collar around the neckline I almost passed out. She was petite and beautiful. She was well at an age now, but she was strong. Everything that I read about or heard spoken about her was true. I remember her dissenting on the Lilly Ledbetter Fair Pay Opinion changing the lives of women workers in America. Her dissent on opinions had paved the way to dismantle gender-based discrimination. She was every woman in America's champion. As the oral arguments began, I said a prayer thanking God for allowing me to honor my niece Keenya Cook. I never wanted her to be forgotten. Now the Supreme Justices would say her name. My life changed on February 16, 2002, when my niece died as the first victim of John Muhammad's wrath and 16-year-old Lee Boyd Malvo's descent. In October 2019 my healing had plateaued at that moment.

As a family member of someone killed by a young person, I promote healing, build advocacy capacity, and develop leadership among "survivor families" who, like me, have lost loved ones to youth violence but are nonetheless interested in challenging the extreme punishment of children. I bring about meaningful, direct support to victims of violence committed by children and systemic change in how we hold young people accountable for the harm they have caused. As I continue this work, I continue to fight for the inclusion of all parties and participants involved that the best possible, most beneficial outcome prevails. This is an outcome where all are offered healing and restoration.

CHAPTER 2

Genesis: Revelation by Revelation

*"Although we may not realize it at the time,
the road to our higher self requires shedding energies
that not no longer serve our highest good."*
~ Schan Ellis Robinson

In the Beginning

To tell this story, I have to tell a story of abuse, rage, and betrayal. It is one of the secrets, depression, and the impeding mental challenge of digesting it all. This is the narrative of family and friendship—a story that starts at the mouth of a raging river, and despite its danger, will eventually deliver me from this pain and lead me to heal. Along that river came a fork, and it was I who had to decide if I would heal and reach pleasant waters or continue to be thrown by the rapids.

I continued to get phone calls from supportive friends. Somewhere along the way, I started to emerge from behind the veil, just a bit, to return some of the calls and eventually to check e-mails. One of those e-mails was from my good friend and former client, Mildred Williams Muhammad. In 1994, Mildred Williams came into my tax office, Nichols-Wright and Associates, which was located in the Hilltop of Tacoma, Washington. I had a bookkeeping, tax preparation, and business-consulting firm. My office was on the main corridor of Martin Luther King Jr. Way in Tacoma. There were two traffic lights on both sides of MLK Way, and my office was between 12th Street and 13th Street. Mildred was driving down MLK Way toward 13th Street when she noticed my accounting office. As she sat there and waited for the light to turn green, she was able to read the services we offered by reading the large advertisement in our window. She sat and waited for the light to change, took her car around the block, found a parking spot, and walked towards my office. I looked out and I saw a spotless, white Nissan 300 ZX sports car, and out of the car come this very charming looking African American female heading into my doorway. She came into the office looking for information regarding our services, and she noticed I was what she called a "Sistah," a term of endearment often used to refer to close female friends in the African American community. I was not expecting any clients that day. I was just doing some data entry I had to catch up on and writing some letters.

When she entered the office, she said, *"Hello."*

I said, *"Hello, how can I help you?"*

She extended her hand, and after we shook she asked, *"You're African American?"*

I responded jokingly, *"Last time I checked."*

We laughed, she introduced herself, and I offered her a seat. Mildred Williams was the owner of a small auto repair business.

RESTORE

Her husband, John Williams, was the mechanic. Mildred is of average height, and her deep complexion contrasted with her beautiful, bright smile. She had her hair wrapped with a beautiful scarf, and I could tell that she was Muslim. Her dress was significant to women of the Muslim faith, who wear attire that cover the hair down to the feet. Mildred began to describe a car and truck repair business she and her husband, John, had started in Tacoma. The business began from their home, and they had only recently moved the business to the Tacoma Small Business Incubator. She also said that their business was growing, and she needed some help with their bookkeeping and accounting. When she saw the advertising in the window, she felt it was a divine moment because she had been praying to Allah to provide resources and support for their growing business.

Mildred was extremely polite. I asked her if she had the proper licensing for their business. She responded with a *"yes, ma'am."* She was so charismatic, formal, and respectful. It emanated from her gestures and within the gaze of her eye.

"If you 'yes ma'am' me one more time, I am going to put you out of my office!" I joked.

We laughed and before she knew it, she had said "yes ma'am" again. I knew then that this was a very nice lady and, of course, I was willing to provide her with a comprehensive business development service package to insure a solid foundation for future financial growth. Nurturing startup businesses is my passion, after all, and it is promising when a client knows enough to seek professional services so their business can be profitable. She mentioned that her husband served in the army as a mechanic and that he was the mechanic for their car repair business. They wanted to start a business that they could operate together and leave as a legacy for their children. The vision she shared with me was something I deeply respected and it was a tangible endeavor.

They had a very unique business concept for repairing cars. Being a mobile car repair service, they went to the customer rather than the customer coming to them. Their creativity intrigued me. I knew that this concept was a niche and with the right type of accounting and business planning, they could become extremely profitable. I gave Mildred a business card and brochure. She was anxious to get home and let her husband know that she had found an African American accountant and business consultant. We set an appointment, and I gave her a checklist of bookkeeping data, along with information that she should provide to begin bookkeeping for her. I let her know to call me if she had any questions or problems, and I emphasized the importance of meeting her husband. I took a holistic approach to my bookkeeping and accounting practice, and I supplied administrative and management services linked with bookkeeping, tax, and accounting services. I expressed to her how important it was to me to be holistically involved.

When Mildred came back for the appointment, we signed a contract and we went over the services that I was going to provide, including monthly bookkeeping, accounting, business, and personal tax preparation, and business consultations. She then paid me a retainer to start our contract. All of the information I requested from our prior meeting she had already organized neatly. It was even in chronological order. She was seemingly meticulous about all details, neat in her presentation, and clearly articulated her ideas to me.

RESTORE

I began to enter the data and gave her a time frame in which I would have the information and have some reporting for her. I again kindly requested that her husband John be in attendance. It was very important for them to use the financial statements as an inspection tool for their business, and that it was my job to train them to use their financial statements. We finally ended the appointment, and Mildred was very ecstatic, gave me that beautiful smile, and embraced me. Her excitement and cheerfulness were contagious, and I was gratified by her reception of my ideas and direction as her accountant and consultant.

When the next appointment came, in walked Mildred and her husband. John Williams was very clean-cut, tall, and very respectful. He introduced himself as Mildred and I embraced, and I asked them to sit down. John was very friendly and was just as excited as his wife in finding an African American owned accounting firm to service their needs. He avidly believed in supporting black businesses in the community and said that "if more black people supported and patronized black businesses, we would be some of the wealthiest citizens in America." I agreed.

I got the reports ready, and I presented a copy of the financial statements to the Williamses. I began to show them the income that was generated, less the cost of the goods or materials purchased, less the expenses, and what their net profit was. Their net profit was small, yet they were still operating with positive cash flow. I began to explain that the balance sheet was an actual picture of the company.

John energetically asked, *"A picture of what?"*

I, of course, was ready with my professional response.

"A picture of the assets, whether cash or inventory and loans; also the liabilities of the company, what the company owed to creditors. Also any liability for accounts payable, and then the capital paid in money you had put into the business yourselves."

Mildred explained that, for the first time, they were able to see the outcomes of their efforts. The numbers supported their hard work put into the business. I also explained that we would analyze the next three months of reports and determine if there was a spending pattern and see what the volume would be. The goal would be to find out how much they were spending in parts for the automobiles, and negotiate with their volume to get better costs for parts, thus reducing their expense and increasing their profit. This was the first strategy that was laid out for *Express Car Truck Mechanic*. *Express Car Truck Mechanic* was a sole proprietorship when they first contracted with me. Every month, Mildred would call to make an appointment. As she had done during our first appointment, she gathered the receipts and organized them with adherence to every detail. She put the receipts in the order that I had them on the financial statements. I was impressed that she paid such attention to detail. Mildred served as the office administrator and dispatcher. She networked to bring in business. She handled all the day-to-day functions. John was the mechanic and would go to appointments every day. Appointments that Mildred had set up. Once a month I would meet with John and Mildred to go over the financial statements, and we would also talk about ways to increase profits and reduce overhead.

From 1994 to 1998 I provided services and consulted John and Mildred in accounting and administration. We started developing a business plan, which included a marketing plan for contract work. The contract work was vital, as it would allow the business not to be solely dependent on just one avenue or method of generating revenue. We identified the industry for fleets that would need servicing like rental cars, trucking businesses, and just about any type of business that had fleet automobiles. We devised a package that was a preventative maintenance package, which eventually became a very lucrative and steady source of income for the included services such as oil, lube, and tune-up at a fixed price for fleet repairs. It increased the profit of *Express Car Truck Mechanic* and in four years went from a sole proprietorship to a corporation. They hired an assistant to help John in the field repairing cars. They also hired an office receptionist and an independent marketing consultant to implement the marketing and sales from the business plan. The consultant's primary role was to go on sales calls to get contracts for car and truck companies.

Mildred transitioned the business into a polished and mainstream corporation in its attire, operations, and look. She ordered uniforms and designed stationary with logos and revamped the branding for the entire company. She had matching letterhead and business cards and had their logo put on the uniforms. She designed their invoices and estimate sheets with the company's logo and branding. Within a few years, *Express Car Truck Mechanic* became a household name. The service was so professional that Mildred had evaluation cards that she gave to clients to rate the service provided. She realized that customer service and care were the vital vehicles to success needed for success in their business. I would always remind them that profit was not made by the sale of the service, but by the return of that client for service. We wanted the clients to come back for more services and to make referrals.

The Muhammad Family –REVELATION OF FRIENDSHIP

John and Mildred had three young children, two girls, and one son. Little John, Salena, and the baby Taalibah. Taalibah was 15 months old when I first met the whole family. Mildred and I began to grow closer, and our families became close as well. My oldest daughter, Tasherra, was a fill-in babysitter for their three children, while Mildred and John worked the business. I celebrate my birthday in April, and since it coincided with the end of the tax season, I would entertain my clients to thank them for their business. I went all out in my birthday celebration, honoring my clients while also networking for new clients. John and Mildred attended. John helped fry the fish for the cookout. We had a good time.

Our relationship had just grown to be so pleasurable that my family was invited to the Williams' family celebrations. I had the privilege of meeting Mildred's mother, Ms. Olivia Green. Ms. Olivia was in her late sixties, and she was the primary caregiver for the Williams children whom she loved dearly. She resided with the family while John and Mildred worked 10 to 12-hour days. Mrs. Green was on social security, and she had some medical illnesses. One of her illnesses, I recall, was diabetes, and was a stroke survivor. Ms. Olivia was a very strong and opinionated, Christian woman. She was not Muslim, and did not waste any time letting you know that she was "Saved, Sanctified, and Filled with the Holy Ghost." When she found out I was a

RESTORE

Christian, she would share with me often the goodness of Jesus Christ.

Ms. Olivia loved her daughter and John whom she looks at like a son, very much. It was Mildred's decision not to allow her mother to be put in a nursing home, but to come and share in her life. It was not always easy as Mildred was raised Christian, and had recently converted to the Nation of Islam. This was quite a change from the Christian child Ms. Olivia raised. she knew very little about Islam or the Nation of Islam. She continued with her faith, praying in the name of Jesus. Mildred respected her mother and made sure that she got to church, prayer meetings, and anywhere else she needed to go.

I, too, had my parent staying with me. My father, James Farrington, was a stroke survivor as well. In 1993, I moved my father to Tacoma with me, to live with my husband Joseph, my daughters, and me. My father's stoke came one week before his 60th birthday. He was retired from 20 years of truck driving. In his spare time, my father was delivering lunches to senior citizens at noon. One day he had got out of his truck and his leg began to drag, and he fell over. Fortunately, someone had seen him fall and noticed that he was having a stroke. The paramedics were called, and he was taken to the hospital. The stroke changed my father's entire life. The quality of his life, as he knew it, was now dependent on help from others. I had always told him I would be there for him whenever he needed me and that I would not abandon him. I told him to always remember that I would care for him. I meant that. Having to care for elderly parents was just another area in life that Mildred and I shared. Both of our parents were demanding and in need. They both had critical medical conditions and we both were the youngest siblings taking care of our elderly parents.

When John would come by the house to do a repair or to do a tune-up, he would talk with my father. My father loved to talk, and the fact that John knew a lot about cars and trucks was intriguing to my father. My father was a retired truck driver, after all. *Express Car Truck Mechanic* repaired my mother in-law's vehicles, my vehicle, my husband's vehicle, or most of our friends. We had referred them to our friends and acquaintances. We had shared their service and their concept with just about everyone we knew who needed car repair service. John and my father would talk for at least an hour, with John entertaining my father with details of makes, engines, and parts. My father would roll his wheelchair to engage John in conversations about trucks. John always called my father "Sir" and would always respond with a "Yes, Sir" and a "No, Sir" much like Mildred. My father admired John as a hard-working businessman with a beautiful family, and he would tell John this as if John was his very own son. My father also enjoyed the company of Mildred too when she visited. My father could never get the names of Mildred and John's daughters correct. After struggling to recall their names, he simply referred to them as the "Sheba's." The Sheba's were in all actuality Salena and Taalibah, and Mildred and I would burst out laughing. When the children were around, they were just as respectful as their parents, with the "No, sirs" and "no ma'ams" ready for us. They were so intelligent and very articulate. They could read even before they went to school. John Jr. was treated as John's second in command. His daughters were referred to as his queens, daddy's African Queens. Mildred was very passionate about her family, and she loved her

RESTORE

husband very much. She wanted the business to be successful. She wanted her husband to be a proud, successful black man in the eyes of the community, his family, and his Mosque. They were devout and dedicated to the Nation of Islam. They worshipped at the Mosque on Sundays, and Mildred even held a district leadership position there. Together they served their Mosque with much dedication and pride.

The *Million Man March* of 1995 that Minister Farrakhan called for in Washington D.C. was like a natural calling to John. Mildred was so proud that he attended, and I was proud that this event was atonement for black men in America — to atone to their families, their mothers, their sisters, and their community. It was not just a Muslim event. Rather it was a call for every black man in America to be present at the nation's capital and make their presence known with pride. Mildred invited me over, and I even decided to not work in my office, and instead watch this historical event in the comfort of her home. I gladly accepted her invitation, and we watched the unfolding of a very historic moment in our African American culture and the world. We shared a sense of solidarity although I was Christian, and I believed in the Trinity, thus believing in Jesus Christ, as the Messiah and Savior. We sat there, from the early hours of the morning to the latter part of the evening. I remember looking through the colored pixels of the television, looking to see a mere spec of John there in the crowd. We knew that this was a time in history when people of all religious beliefs were coming together. We watched the most powerful display of black men. Something that just had not been heard of before. There was not a single criminal activity, nor was there the behavior society stereotyped as being "black." This was true empowerment, strength, and poise. They did a demonstration of how powerful our economic power in this country by asking every black man to hold up a one-dollar bill. They asked that every person pass the dollar to the next man behind them. We watched on television as over a million men passed at least a million dollars through everyone's hands. Mildred and I sat there, holding each other's hands, looking at this exercise of economic power going through our black men's hands. We held hands and were speechless at the power that exuded from the screen that day. When John returned from the *Million Man March*, I wanted to hear everything John had to say. I wished that my husband Joseph could have attended. He was away in Korea, but he had watched the *Million Man March* broadcasted there. I often wondered if Joseph was here in America would he have made the journey to Washington, D.C. to experience the March. Would it have made a difference in his life? Did he have that sense of purpose, as a provider and as a breadwinner? Would he be willing to atone for his mistreatment of me? Would it have deposited something in him that could be of value? I would have paid anything to get him there, to even feel that pride that Mildred must have felt when John returned. Instead, I was left questioning my relationship with my man.

From 1994 until 1998, *Express Car Truck Mechanic* had grown. They were now doing annual sales in the six digits with just one mechanic and a couple of assistants. I filed their reports and taxes, making sure that they understood everything. I made sure that John and Mildred understood the importance of paying sales tax and income taxes so that the tax agencies would not have to be a problem. Many African American businesses would make the mistake of co-mingling sales taxes with operations and

RESTORE

when it was time to pay, they did not have the money. I did not want *Express Car Truck Mechanic* to fall into this same trap. Unfortunately, after some time, John began missing appointments and the financial statements started to reveal inconsistencies in parts purchased and cash received. One day, Mildred received a disturbing phone call from a female client. She was asking to speak to the owner of the company. Most people thought that John was an employee because he had a uniform with his name sewn on a patch. He looked as if he was just another employee. Mildred made all calls and appointments, and when this particular call came in, Mildred explained that she was the owner, and the woman began to complain that John was stalking her and soliciting her for sex. She wanted to file a complaint and was considering suing *Express Car Truck Mechanic* for the misconduct of their employee, John Williams. Somewhere between that march in Washington and Mildred's utter shock, the Williamses began to have problems in their business and apparently their marriage. Mildred called me, and the confusion I sensed in the paperwork was manifested in her tone. Clients were saying that they had paid John in cash but Mildred never saw the cash or any deposits of cash into the business account. When Mildred confronted John about the phone call, he denied it and said that the woman was trying to pay him with sexual favors for fixing her car. He was angry that this woman had called and made up a lie. He resented the speculation from this complaint. Mildred contracted a marketing professional that had extensive experience in sales and marketing. He had worked for Fortune 500 companies, and maybe he could salvage the company's reputation after this accusation. He had received awards and was recognized for his sales volume and expertise.

He was also a good friend of John and Mildred. He was very professional in his attire and was a Christian man who was ethical and well-spoken. Mildred had asked if he would follow-up on the woman's complaint. His concern spurred his rapid interest in mediating this matter before it got out of control. He called the client and made arrangements to meet with her to further investigate her complaint. Nonetheless, things continued to get worse.

John continued to miss appointments. He was showing signs of resentment and speculation around the business' rapid growth. Mildred even told me that John was not in places where he needed to be, and she did not know of his whereabouts at certain times. There were times when John didn't come home until the next day. Things just weren't adding up in the spreadsheets or their home, and I could not help but wonder how their balance sheets in life and business had become so inconsistent. With John being the only mechanic, this affected the company's ability to generate revenue. It affected the ability of their household to be supported. Bills began to pile, both at home and at the business. It was the first time in four years that Mildred could no longer afford to pay for my services. I just could not abandon her at this time. It was my feeling that this was just going to be a short phase, and they would get back on track with things. Accounts and balances could be salvaged if only there is the intention, energy, and will to do so.

I provided Mildred with instructions on how to continue the record keeping. She already had a system in place for managing record-keeping on her own. She could come in and get their annual reports or even file quarterly. The main burden of paying for record-keeping was now no longer an issue, and she was able to keep me on an as-needed basis. I continued to support Mildred with consulting on some of the business problems, but the problems continued to multiply. When a strong imbalance presents itself, it tends to be like a black hole that sucks away everything that you could potentially put into it. Even if your investment is pure intentioned. Something drastic had to be done, for what was once a six-figure business was in the red. What seemed like a happy and proud family was suddenly not so.

I made a lot of adjustments in my business and my practice. I ended a four-year business partnership with my partner Tony Wright, and I was no longer Nichols-Wright and Associates, but Nichols and Associates. I no longer had an office. Instead, I worked from home to be available to my family. From 2000 to 2001, I did not hear very much from Mildred or her family. I too was going through some transition in my life. I had been separated from my husband, and in 1999 he had returned from duty in Korea. We decided to reconcile and put our family back together. In 2000 I began to re-focus my energy on the reconciliation of my marriage. Just as Mildred realized some gaping holes in her life, I realized that I wanted more than anything for my marriage to work. For the first time, I put my marriage before everything, making it a priority. I felt I needed to show my husband that he was a priority. I wanted him to know that I loved and respected him.

The American Dream – REVELATION OF BETRAYAL

Nichols and Associates were the only African American, independent, public accountants in the Tacoma, Pierce County area and I was expanding again. I was interested in growing my business and diversifying into other areas. I wanted to get into residential mortgage lending. Tax season was ending and the time was good for me to look into that industry. Tax planning and home ownership were becoming more appealing to me. Joseph and I were separated and were living in two separate homes. Although we were only separated by location, we continued to care for one another. We would sleep together. That part of the marriage was not one of our issues. This went on for years. For some reason, it did not bother me. Whenever I needed Joseph, he would be there. Often he would be there when I hadn't even called. We were really good friends. We loved each other, and we knew that. We loved our children even more. Neither one of us ever mentioned divorce. I conducted my life as the wife of Joseph Nichols despite our 'married but separate' lifestyle. In 1997, I found a beautiful new home that was for sale by the owner. I even qualified to buy the home, but to get a better interest rate and loan to value ratio, I needed to show more income. I asked Joseph if he would sign onto the documents so that I could include his income. I asked him to meet me at the house so that he could see it. I convinced him that the girls and I needed a home. We both could purchase homes and leave them each a home. Joseph loved our daughters. He would do anything for them.

The loan program that I was qualifying for was conventional. Joseph could use his VA as a veteran to get himself a home later. Joseph did not think that I could afford the house, and I let him know that I had started a new contract that was paying me $5,000 per month. I reminded him that his financial support for the girls would be used. The strategy made sense to him, and he agreed to sign the documents. The loan closed escrow in October of 1997 and my daughters, my father, and I moved into our new home. Things were going according to plan. I wished I had my husband there to share with me the joys of buying a new home, of having something for us and our children. I hoped we could building memories there together, choosing where to place the couch, maybe even preparing a meal together there in a new kitchen.

In 1998 Joseph went back to Korea for a one-year Army tour of duty. It was his third Korean assignment. While he was abroad we started talking about our family. He said he wanted to come back home. Although I was nervous, I did want him back. I still loved him. I believed that God could do anything, and that included healing broken marriages. I believed I could do anything through Christ strengthening me. When his tour of duty was over we decided that he would come home to me and our girls. In October of 1999, Joseph and I reunited from a four-year marital separation. We were now just about in our 40's. I believed that Joseph's desire to party all the time had run its course. It had run its course for quite a little while. I could forgive the infidelities. I had done so many times in the past. Forgiveness is a gift. I was gifted when it came to forgiveness. Healing, on the other hand, was not something I knew how to do.

The millennium New Year was approaching and I looked forward to what the year would bring. I did not enter into a new year without setting some goals and expectations. I would pray to God for His will to be manifest in my life. I would pray for myself, for God to continue to strengthen me. I had not spent a new year with Joseph in a few years. Whatever he wanted to do was going to be all right with me. In the past, I would be at the watch meeting service at church. I loved being there. Joseph wanted to go to a party, and yes, I went, however, I wanted to be at the watch service. Partying on a New Year's Eve just did not interest me anymore. The word of God requires a wife to be of the world to attend to the need of her husband, and so I reasoned with myself that this party was something I had to do. I had a lot to thank God for. In the year 2000, I was going to do whatever my husband wanted to do. Since he had just come back from Korea, he wanted to go to a small house gathering with his family and friends. We often partied a lot with my in-laws. They loved to party, and there was no excuse needed to throw one. I dressed up in some good looking clothes. I even did the salon thing, so my hair was on point. My nails were manicured, and my feet were freshly painted and pedicured. I had bought a little negligee for when we got home. I wanted this New Year to be special. When the midnight hour came, I made my way to where Joseph was. I stared at him as he was hollering and counting down. When midnight hit I turned with my eyes closed to wait to kiss him. When I opened my eyes he had left me standing there. I was devastated. The New Year came in with disappointments and it didn't stop that night he left me hanging. Later in the year, I lost my $5,000 per month paying contract, my father became very ill, and he had to move into a nursing home which took his income with him. The financial woes were back, and Joseph was back to his disappearing acts.

We had managed to get our eldest daughter away to attend college at St. Augustine's College in Raleigh, North Carolina. That got my attention. Since I had lost my contract and the income that came from my father was going to the nursing home, I needed to re-think some stuff out. We reluctantly entered into our second bankruptcy, so the house and property tax payments were being paid through it. Joseph was depressed and angry most of the time. It was the typical glass empty versus glass full scenario. I thought the Chapter 13 Bankruptcy was a good resource to have. I was grateful to God that we had something valuable to save through bankruptcy. Yet Joseph was disgusted and embarrassed about the Chapter 13 Bankruptcy. He was appalled that it was our second time. To Joseph, it was my entire fault. Joseph blamed me for our financial problems. It was my fault that we did not have any savings. It was my fault that we had filed two bankruptcies. It was my fault that he didn't have the rank he wanted. I was not the woman he wanted to come home to, so he didn't come home. There were times when I had to look in the closet to make sure he had not moved out. I was not the type of woman that would go on a stakeout to find out where my husband was or who he was with. I didn't have that kind of time. I had my daughters, and I was very much involved in their lives. I had the comfort of my beautiful home and my children. I shared with my husband that I wanted to expand my business to include mortgage lending. His reactions were the same as usual. He was not interested. Here he was at Fort Lewis with hundreds of soldiers and did very little to send business my way. Imagine the VA loan lending potential. I could never get Joseph to understand that any of my businesses were worthwhile. It could be better if I had his support. If I wasn't bringing home a paycheck every two weeks, then it did not carry any value to him. He compared me often to female soldiers. He respected them because they went to work every day. He respected any female that went to work on an "8 to 5" every day. He just did not value entrepreneurialism. He made me aware of it every chance he could.

Whenever I would ask Joseph anything about his whereabouts he would tell me *"it was none of my business."* If I asked him for money for bills he would say that *"when I started making some money, then I could ask him for some."* He could be verbally abusive and cold-hearted. When he wanted to insult me he would call me a dumb ass. He knew I had two Bachelor's degrees, so dumb ass was when he really wanted to get me angry which gave him a reason to leave the house. Joseph was gone four days a week at night clubs or hanging out with "the fellas." To this day, I don't know what grown man would want to hang out with the guys until 4 and 5 AM. Yet I do know one thing. Infidelity is expensive. I knew that he was out with other women. That was why he never had any savings. I was not the type to let anyone know that I was struggling to keep the marriage together. When he came home he was wreaking with alcohol. It was just prayer and the grace of God that he made it home. I would always be awake. I never could sleep when he wasn't home. I worried about him being out there in the streets.

During the fall of October 2001, I got a job, the kind he wanted me to have. I wanted to see if it would make a difference in Joseph's behavior. Would it bring him home at night? Would I get his respect? Nope! I started work for All Fund Mortgage in Spanaway, Washington as a contract loan processor. Pamela Martinez was the branch manager. Pamela had a white girl sounding voice, a Hispanic last name, but she was a dark-skinned, beautiful, African American female. It was a family run business. Naturally, this impressed me. I interviewed with Pamela, and I was hired. I went into training as a processor and loan officer. I didn't let anyone know of my experience in accounting, or that I had a tax practice. It was all about learning the residential mortgage industry. I was excited to be on their team. Pamela knew her business. She had the business savvy and worked long hours. This quality we both had. I wanted to know what she knew about the business so I listened to every word she said. I believe in surrounding myself with positive people. I mirrored her even to the point that I started wearing these cute pony tails like her. They were neat and convenient. I was always a low maintenance kind of person anyway. Pamela's office was predominately white. Her mother, Ms. Frankie, and her sister were the only African American women I saw most of the time. I was impressed by a "Sistah girl" running her business with predominately white staff.

    I was having a blast. On the homefront things were stable. My niece, Keenya, had just recently moved in with us with her five-month-old baby girl. My home was a refuge to many. One afternoon, I stopped by to see Mildred out of the clear blue. She just popped in my spirit and heart. I happened to be in the neighborhood when I decided to stop in. I pulled into the driveway, and I saw the front door open. I walked up and knocked on the door. I saw a silhouette of her and a man standing in the house. I knocked on the door, and Mildred answered. She asked me to come in and was quite surprised. I had not seen her in about a year. Mildred was in her house with her brother. Her brother stopped by from time to time, as he was a truck driver. Whenever he was in town, he would make it a point to stop in and check on his sister, his mother, and the family.

    I noticed how strange it was that the children were not running around to greet me. It was quiet. It was very quiet. I asked Mildred where the children were. Then there was this stare she gave me. When I asked her where the children were again, she looked very worried. It was as if a bad spirit had invaded this home and taken with it all the joy and eloquence I used to see in Mildred's face. She slowly began to tell me that John had taken her babies and that he was supposed to have brought them home hours ago. My immediate response was, when are they coming back? I was going to sit down as I had some time to kill and did not think much of what she had said. John was just running late or out doing something. But I realized the distress in her face, and the energy of the room was ominous. I asked her what she meant by "supposed to bring them home." Mildred explained to me that it was Ms. Olivia's birthday and that John had picked the children up from school. The last thing she told John was to bring the children back so they could have cake and ice cream for their grandmother's birthday. He agreed, but it was now many hours beyond birthday cake and songs, and she did not hear anything from them. Her brother had to leave and told his sister he would give her a call, and Mildred and I sat in the living room. I was in shock as she revealed the types of threats she was receiving from John. She began to share with me why she was concerned. Mildred looked so fearful. I immediately got the impression that something was wrong. I didn't want to leave Mildred. I asked how Ms. Olivia was doing, and she said that she was okay, but she, too, was worried about the children. As we sat there, waiting to hear anything, looking at the telephone to see if it would ring, wondering and hoping that John would call to say that he was on his way, Mildred began to explain to me the events of their separation. I learned that Mildred and John had separated in the early part of 2000. He was no longer living in their home. John was coming to get his children for weekend visitations that were not mandated by the court but were just arranged between him and Mildred during the separation. In February of 2000, John had tried to enter their home to see their son because he was sick. She had told him that he could not see him because he was asleep, however, John pushed his way into the house and pushed her out of the way. She then ran back and called 911. When the police arrived, they said there was nothing they could do without a restraining order. Mildred went on to explain to me so many crazy things, so many peculiar things that John was doing. She mentioned that before that incident, John came to the house around 7 a.m. to inform her that he had tapped the phone lines. He had said that the information he had would destroy her. She said he started threatening her and from then on she began to feel extremely unsafe. Then the following day after the police had come, he came over and this time he was informing her that he would not let her raise their children. This is exactly the next day after she called 911 to file a complaint.

Now, I understood why Mildred was so intense and fearful. I understood why she felt that something was wrong. The only thing I could think of was to have her notify the police if she felt that John had done something with the children. I asked her if there was a restraining order, and she informed me that she had filed a restraining order with the court. I told her that was probably one of the best things she could have done because, with John's irrational behavior, the threats needed to be on the record. John repeatedly violated the restraining order from February. As Mildred continued to recount her nightmare, she stated that she went again in March to file another restraining order because John was still threatening and calling to destroy her life. She informed the court that she had to change her telephone number three times within 5 days and that she had spoken with a representative at U.S. West Communications, the telephone company. Their representative said that, according to their records, John called that day trying to find out her phone number. The telephone company sympathized with Mildred and had a special code on her phone records. Because of that code, John wasn't able to get the number. Mildred again told the court that she was afraid of John. She said that John was a demolition expert in the military and that he was behaving very irrationally. Whenever he talked to her, he said that he was going to destroy her life, and then he would hang up the phone.

Now here we were sitting in her living room, thinking the worst of the worst. I tried to strategize and give Mildred resources as to what she could do as we waited for the telephone to ring, to see if John was going to bring the children back. It was now well after 8:00 pm and there was still no word from John nor the children. Unfortunately, John never brought the children home that night. As I went home to my own family, there was such a nervous and empty feeling in my stomach regarding the possibility that John had taken their children, Mildred's children. After hearing the dissolution of their marriage, and hearing the hopeless, sordid details of their destroyed home, after learning of the harassment and the constant threats, I was greatly concerned. I began to pray for their safety, that there would be an explanation we could all understand, that somehow those children would be home. I felt that John would just be playing a mean game to scare Mildred into letting him come back and be with her.

I got a call from Mildred the next morning. She had contacted the police. John had called later on that evening and said that he and the children had been at K-Mart shopping. He was getting them something to eat and would be bringing them home

RESTORE

shortly. John never returned with the children. Three days later, John still failed to show up, nor call about his whereabouts or the children. Mildred began to get together more information. She found out that the children's savings accounts were closed, and that John had taken the money out of each child's account. Each child had about $300 or so dollars. She also found out that John had contacted the landlord and told him that he was no longer living there, and was no longer responsible for the rent payments on the house. She reported to the police that her children were missing, and provided the police with pictures of the children. She contacted the school that the children attended to find out what time the children were picked up. The school confirmed the time and confirmed that their father picked them up. Mildred later discovered a real blow. The police could not do much because John was the father, and just because the children were in his care, was not in violation of any type of law since there was no custody agreement. I stressed the importance of her to get an attorney so that she could find out exactly what her rights were. I could not understand how he could have rights to the children at the expense of her rights. I developed a huge WHY factor:

- ❖ Why could they not at least bring the children in and let the courts decide, or put them in foster care until the courts could decide the custodial plan for these children?
- ❖ Why couldn't the authorities take Mildred's statement that these children were taken and that she had not heard from them?
- ❖ Why was that not enough to start an investigation?

- ❖ Why couldn't they bring them into protective custody and let John and Mildred go before the judge to get their parenting issues handled?

No one should have rights at the expense of the other. Mildred's twist of horror only continued. She eventually got a notice of eviction from the landlord. I asked her how far behind she was in the payment. I happened to have some money in my savings. I contacted the landlord and told him that I could catch the payment up, but he would not accept it. He said that he wanted to sell the property, and therefore, he denied our request to let Mildred live in the house. Mildred and I both pleaded with the landlord, telling him that John had taken the children, and telling him how important it would be that she remains there because that was the last known address the children knew. The children knew their entire address including zip code and they also knew the telephone number. To no avail, he proceeded with his request for her to vacate his property. I began to tell Mildred to stay in the house as long as she could while looking for some place else, that the eviction process was not something that would occur in a couple of days, but about three or four weeks. That was as much time as she would have before the eviction would be final in court. Hopefully, within that time, John would show up with the kids. I prayed that the WHY factor would diminish on its own.

Life Interrupted – MY REVELATION OF MISPLACED DEVOTION

Our conversations always began with, *"Have you heard from John about the children?"*

RESTORE

It was hard to believe that John had done this, especially done this to his children. I wanted to believe that this was just one giant misunderstanding or just an immature and misdirected outlet of temporary anger. Either way, the agony was taking its toll on everyone. Not only did pain and mania consume Mildred, but Ms. Olivia was feeling the effects of her grandchildren missing. John had spoken with her and made comments that he was going to destroy her daughter. She had to awaken every day and see the fearful, morbid look on her baby girl's face. She was afraid that John would follow through on the many threats he made about destroying Mildred. She had every right to be fearful. She lived in the home and witnessed most of John's violent, aggressive, and abusive treatment of her daughter.

Over time financial resources were getting thinner. Mildred had no income. John had taken all the money. Ms. Olivia lived off her social security benefits, which wasn't a whole lot. As a mother, she was going to be there for her daughter. She made sure that they had necessities. I tried to do whatever I could do to support and sustain them. My financial resources were not that great either. I would give $30 or $40 to help with her bills or whatever she needed it for. Financial issues were big issues in my marriage just as well. I just prayed that my husband would understand. When I told him what was going on with Mildred, he was supportive. He didn't appear to be irritated. It somehow took my mind off of my marital problems. As Mildred's eviction quickly approached something had to be done. Where were they going to go? How were the children going to contact home? It was the only home that the children knew how to reach. Mildred, Ms. Olivia, and I prayed without ceasing. Mildred prayed to Allah. Ms. Olivia and I prayed in Jesus' name for a miracle. I don't know how

Muslims feel about miracles, but I knew then that God was a miracle maker, and we needed one soon.

It was now early May 2001. I had a client named Patricia that was a mental health professional with her own practice. I was worried because one of the children's birthday was approaching. I contacted Patricia. Patricia told me to bring Mildred to the office. Patricia sat with Mildred and me, and I listened as Mildred related John's actions to Patricia. Patricia listened intently. Patricia's children had been taken away from her by their father as well. She shared her story of what she did to cope until she got them back. She suggested that Mildred should continue to celebrate the children's birthday — that she should buy gifts and wrap them so that when they returned, they would see that she hadn't forgotten about them. I thought that was a wonderful idea.

Patricia was focused on Mildred's coping strategy. She was confident that Mildred would be reunited with her children. It struck me just how many women could share a story of being denied their babies. Patricia was an angel with wings that day for me. I offered to pay Patricia for her services, but she provided the consultation pro-bono for Mildred. Patricia encouraged us to stay in contact with her, and she wanted to see Mildred again. The next thing I knew Mildred had developed a website where she had scanned the latest school pictures of her children on there. She had also gotten an 800 number and a pager so anyone could contact her 24/7 with information about her children. Now her children were on the world wide web as missing children. Mildred had to ask herself each day the same questions. What and where would she be when her children are found?

- Would she be ready to step in and take them?

RESTORE

- ➢ Would she be in shock?
- ➢ Would they receive her openly?
- ➢ Would she be healthy?
- ➢ What would she need to do to keep them safe?

    Mother's Day was approaching. I constantly reminded her that she had to take care of herself. I noticed she wasn't eating and no longer had an appetite. Mildred was anemic. At her office, she fainted and had to be taken to the hospital. All I could think about was how difficult it was going to be for Mildred to wake up on Mother's Day without her children. When seeing another going through an ordeal that is beyond us, we feel unqualified or even stupid for asking questions that truly have no answers. How could I ask how was she doing? How would I be if one day my children were gone, vanished without a trace? All I could do was pray that they were protected and brought back safely. When it was finally Mother's Day, and I was getting ready to go to church with my family, the telephone rang. It was Ms. Olivia. She said that she needed my help. She asked me to go to the emergency room at St. Joseph's Hospital. Mildred was taken there by ambulance. I asked if she wanted me to come and pick her up and she firmly said, *"No, I need you to go!"*

    I will never forget the fear in her voice as she pleaded with me to go. I told her I would get over to the hospital right away and told my husband that I would just meet him and my daughter at church. He knew something was wrong, cautioned me to calm myself, and to drive carefully. I asked him to pray. He said that he would. When I arrived at the emergency room, Mildred was on a gurney in a small room behind a curtain. I went inside the room behind the curtain. Our eyes met, and then she began to cry. She started apologizing to me for not taking care of herself. She said that she tried. As tears filled her big eyes, she took on the look of her youngest baby girl, Taalibah. I began to stroke her head gently. We both were crying. We cried tears of fear, defeat, and frustration. Once I was able to get my composure I tried to console her. I had to let her know that she was taking the best care of herself that she could. I commended her and told her how proud I was of her. I told her that I loved her. I told her that I would be there for her, and we were going to get through this. Mildred told me that there was a knock at her front door. She answered the door to find the postman there to deliver a package to Ms. Olivia. It was sent by one of her sisters for Mother's Day. The postman gave her a clipboard to sign for the package. The next thing she knew she was in an ambulance. The postman told the ambulance personnel that after signing for the package she fell back on the floor hitting her head very hard. He then ran back to his jeep to get his cell phone and dialed 911. Ms. Olivia came to the front and saw her daughter lying on the floor. The postman explained to her what had happened. The ambulance arrived and got her to the hospital. Just as she was finishing up recounting the events, the nurse came to check on Mildred and said that she was going out to take some x-rays. They felt she may have had a concussion from the fall. She said that they would next have to run blood tests after the x-rays. I decided to stay until it was time for her to go. Suddenly the curtains were whisked back and entered this woman. She was dressed in Muslim attire typical of the Nation of Islam. She walked in front of me as if I was invisible. She didn't say excuse me nor hello. I just stood there in curiosity. She bent over to Mildred and asked, *"Beloved, how are you?"* I was standing there in awe when Mildred introduced me as her friend and said that they worship at the same mosque. She finally said hello. She continued to talk to Mildred and acted as if I wasn't there. Her lack of eye contact, her stiff movements, the distance she created in the room was not bringing any positive energy. It was as if she was waiting for me to leave the room, but I wasn't going anywhere. I had to see what this spirit was about. Mildred began to explain to her what little she remembered. I wasn't going to give up any information. Her countenance was all wrong. I just waited quietly, watching her every move. My spirit just made me stay put. She kept asking Mildred all kinds of questions like had she heard from John? Mildred told her that someone kept calling the house and hanging up. She felt it was John. I remember Mildred sharing with me that she had gone to her sisters at the mosque for help and support during some of the most difficult times in her marriage. She felt that she and John needed counseling. I don't remember her saying that she received any. John went to the elders at the mosque and told them that Mildred was not a good wife and that she was having an affair. Mildred later informed me that John had wiretapped the telephone line and tape-recorded a telephone conversation that she had with a male friend. John took the tape to the mosque and played it to them. They believed him because she was removed from a position that she had held in the organization. They had begun to align themselves with John, and they believed his accusations. I didn't understand how the organization would take such a drastic position based on an accusation. I didn't know much about the Nation of Islam other than my exposure with the Muhammad's practicing in it. I knew of some other Muslims in the community. A few were business clients of mine. I did know one thing: This sister's rudeness came through loud and clear, and her constant questioning made me a bit skeptical about her intentions.

ISA FARRINGTON-NICHOLS

The nurse came back to get Mildred and take her for x-rays and a CAT scan. I told Mildred that I would return later after church. Her friend left in the same spirit in which she appeared. I walked down the hospital corridor with Mildred. I called Ms. Olivia and told her that Mildred was stable. I assured her that Mildred was not in any immediate danger, and she was being cared for. Ms. Olivia was traumatized with worry, and I asked her if I should come by, but she refused. I left the hospital and went to join my family.

I finally arrived at church and went in to be seated next to my family. I was exhausted. I was emotionally overwhelmed. My church was having a Mother's Day program and I took a glance at all the mothers in the church. There were mothers like Mildred that did not know where their children were. I looked at my beautiful daughter. I was so proud of both my girls. I then looked at my husband. I stared at him for a little while. Although we were in turmoil trying to make our marriage work, he had not reached that point of darkness to ever sever our children away from me. I thank God for that. While he could be emotionally abusive, we did not involve our girls. I seldom exposed any one of them to my emotional pain and suffering. I just didn't. I often prayed to God to restore our marriage. I prayed that He would touch our hearts, heal our hurts, and change our habits. I knew of no other way to endure difficult times, other than prayer. Prayer changes things. Prayer can get into places where no one else can. That is what I believe. On the way home I shared what I had experienced. By the time that I finished, we all felt sorrowful about the situation. We arrived home and began my Mother's Day celebration. My husband prepared dinner. My daughters had lavished me with gifts and their love. I enjoyed the rest of my

RESTORE

Sunday feeling whole. I was a mother, just as Mildred remained a mother, even if her children were not there with her. As the evening arrived, I called the hospital to check on Mildred. They informed me that she had been admitted to the fifth floor. I decided to leave my family and go back to visit Mildred. When I got to her room, she had I.V.'s running out of her arm, however, she looked much better. The doctor told her that was extremely dehydrated, and her blood pressure was low. Her blood count was anemic. Mildred had been given three pints of blood to help her ailing body, and she spoke her truth to the doctors to help her ailing heart. She said that she had told her doctors about her turmoil and I was glad that she had confided in them.

I knew Mildred needed some serious, professional help, and now she could get some referrals from the medical staff. I was hoping that she could get access to the hospital's psychiatrist and social workers. I asked her if she wanted to seek counseling. She said she hadn't considered it. This episode was an eye-opener. She could no longer go on bearing any more questions or threats anymore. I was convinced that this was not going to get any better—and so far, John's threat of destroying her life was working. Mildred could not take care of herself, let alone take care of her ailing mother. The eviction was just ahead. Mildred was now too sick to get a job yet she needed income. Mildred knew that Ms. Olivia could be stubborn and would not want to move. I asked Mildred if she had contacted her other sisters. One lived in Texas, and one lived in Maryland. Mildred called her sisters. She too realized that she needed to get her mother to live with one of them. She had a lot of things to consider, a lot of things to figure out. The hospital's social worker did come to speak with Mildred and I was relieved of some of the pressures of worrying.

Hysterical and Homeless – THE REVELATION OF MY OWN BROKENESS

On Monday morning I woke up with much anxiety. I had a full day of business clients to serve, a home to run, and a teenage daughter who needed my care. I got on my knees and started talking to my God. I had to thank Him first and foremost for allowing me to see another day. The more I talked to God the lighter I felt, so I stayed there in His presence for a while longer. I didn't want to get up until I knew God had restored me with strength and courage to face the day. I'm still this way today. I don't move until God says so. After prayer, I called Ms. Olivia to see how she was doing. She still did not want to go up to the hospital to see Mildred because she was tired. I asked her if she had been taking her medication, and she said that she had. Ms. Olivia assured me that she and Mildred were going to be okay. She thanked me for my prayers and for being a woman of God. I thanked her too for being kind and loving to me. She asked me if I was going back up to the hospital. She seemed relieved when I said yes.

I arrived at the hospital to find Mildred sitting up in bed. She was still receiving IV fluids in her arm. She looked very well and rested. The blood transfusion had brought her pale skin back to her vibrant skin color. I sat down, and as we began to talk, the telephone rang. She answered it.

"John please let me speak to them! Why are you keeping the children from me? They need their mother. Please!"

Mildred began to cry. Her screams became hysterical with every indignation he deposited.

"No! No! No! John, No!"

Mildred was screaming so loudly the nursing staff came running in. She was kicking and screaming. The I.V. came out of her arm. They looked at me for answers. I was standing there with my mouth open and tears in my eyes, and looked back at them, without words or even a whimper to express my shock. They asked me again what happened. I said it was her husband on the phone. He had taken her children away, and no one has helped her get them back. Mildred continued screaming, "He is going to kill me! He is coming; he is coming to kill me! No, no, don't let him kill me! He is going to kill my mother!" Mildred was crying and so hysterical that they put in an order for a sedative. The hospital staff took the threats seriously and immediately called the Tacoma Police Department. They also moved her to another room on another floor. They took her name off the patient directory. It was apparent that someone had contacted John and told him where Mildred was. I never asked Mildred how her friend knew she was here in the hospital.

They posted hospital security outside her hospital door. All visitors had to sign in and show picture identification. The police arrived and took Mildred's statement on what happened. This was not the first complaint she filed against John. She had filed at least two restraining orders previously with the department for this same type of harassment and threats against her life. This time, the police were more inclined to hear the complaint. She told them everything he said. They sent a patrol car out to her house to check on Ms. Olivia. Ms. Olivia told them that John had called her and threatened to kill her daughter. After constantly asking the police for help, her meeting with Patricia, her website, her pleas to many friends who knew John, the missed birthdays, and Mother's day, the police were going to issue a warrant for his arrest. If Mildred had not ultimately been on a hospital bed to receive that call in an institution of health and medicine, would the police have felt obligated to issue a warrant?

I stayed with her as the medication started to calm her. At the time the only people that knew she was in there was her mother, her friend from the mosque, and myself. I asked Mildred who else she may have called, and she said she called the ministry to get some type of security for herself, known as the FOI. She said she had spoken to a husband of a sister. Someone must have told John that Mildred was here. They must have known how to reach him. Mildred said that John even knew she had received three pints of blood.

I found it difficult to understand how she thought that the people that refused to provide her marital support and removed her from her position would lift a finger to help her and the children. Mildred went to many of them asking if they had seen John with the children. They told her no. They were aware of her accusations against John and they were aware of how he took the children from her. What could Mildred have possibly done to make her friends turn their backs on her? Someone in their ministry should have tried to restore this family. Why was I the only one helping her anyways? I stayed at the hospital most of the day. I called and rescheduled appointments that I had. I was already exhausted, and my day hadn't got underway yet!

The hospital social worker came in to talk to Mildred about her discharge and her safety. She was interested in finding out what would be best for Mildred. Mildred was extremely fragile. She was emotional, withdrawn, and in need of care. Mildred looked at the social worker as if she was in a bubble trying to communicate. I told the social worker that she didn't have any money, any place to live, or any protection. I asked what she recommended. I didn't want to sound cynical, but I wanted to know if there was anything that she could do. The social worker didn't have much at the time. She said she was going to make some phone calls and get back to us.

    The next day when the social worker came back, she had some resources. She recommended putting Mildred in a shelter. They felt she would be safe, and could stay until she could afford to get a place. The shelter was located in Enumclaw, Washington. Enumclaw was a distance of about forty miles from Tacoma. The social worker had contacted the shelter, and they could take Mildred in. She also made arrangements for Mildred to have a police escort to the shelter. Enumclaw was too far away for me in case of an emergency. Mildred did not have any money, and her mother needed care. I mentioned it and the social worker gave me a look as if to say, "*You should be thankful for what I'm offering.*"

    I was thankful, but she didn't know Mildred as I did. She didn't know that leaving Tacoma would devastate Mildred because she needed to look for her children here. Tacoma was the last place she had seen her children. What if they made it back and she was in Enumclaw? I asked Mildred about her mother. She had not spoken to her that day. I suggested that she get on the phone with her sister so that she could come and get their mother as soon as possible.

ISA FARRINGTON-NICHOLS

Mary E. East and The *Phoebe House* – MY REVELATION OF MY NETWORK AND NET WORTH

Mrs. Mary East was about 5'10 with a full figure. She was a strong, beautiful African American woman who had raised two children in Tacoma as a single mother. She was well educated, attending college to receive a nursing degree later becoming a registered nurse. She was a gentle giant in the community and was actively involved in ministry. She was a licensed missionary and known to many in the spiritual community as Missionary East. Mrs. East cared for homeless seniors in her own home. When I first met her she was cooking full course meals in her kitchen and taking them to downtown Tacoma to feed the homeless. She didn't prepare just soup and sandwiches; she cooked chicken, vegetables, beans, cornbread, salad, and dessert from the trunk of her car.

Lines of people would form to eat her food. She would pray with them, and tell them about the goodness of God. God was right there for them, manifesting in the aroma of her hot food and her generosity. Sometimes when the Holy Spirit moved upon her, she would sing a hymn. She had a melodic voice that could pierce through the coldest of hearts.

As the social worker and Mildred discussed the possibility of moving her to a shelter forty miles away, I remembered Mrs. East. She was the Founder and Executive Director of the Phoebe House Association established here in Tacoma for women and their children. Amid my thoughts and worries, I had forgotten that I sit on their board of directors.

I told Mildred I would contact Mrs. East when I got home. It was evening, and I would have to call Mrs. East at her home.

RESTORE

Mildred looked at me with her big eyes and managed to get a smile out. The smile got wider and wider. There was some hope for the seemingly hopeless.

Mrs. East had seen many women and had heard many stories. She was intently listening to mine. She had spent many years of her life feeding the homeless and caring for the elderly, and now homeless women and their children. Her passion for helping women is a gift. Her clean and sober shelters have been home to many women in the Tacoma, Pierce County community. When I returned home, I immediately called Mrs. East. She was glad to hear from me. I told her I needed her help for my friend. I told her all the horrid details of Mildred's experiences. I continued to tell her about the missing children and the elderly mother. I paused to get a response. She sighed. She said that both *Phoebe Houses* were full. My heart sunk.

The Phoebe Houses can accommodate up to 36 women with small children. Not once did it occur to me that the Phoebe House would be full. I asked Mrs. East if she was sure. She said she would make a call. I prayed to God that something would be available. It was the perfect solution. The Phoebe House had an excellent transitional program. There was case management, assessments, and counseling. They had programs that supported self-sufficiency. They provided a myriad of resources and referrals to other social and community-based organizations. They were the best advocates for women that I knew. There was only one thing: Mrs. East ran a strict operation.

She had that reputation and many court judges mandated women there on probation, as opposed to jail, because of the policies and guidelines. The program was an 18-month program and most of the women stayed the entire time. There was always a waiting list to get into the Phoebe House. There were no other programs in Tacoma, let alone Pierce County, that let you stay that long. If you were fortunate enough to get in, you could finish your schooling and even go to college. I know some women who went on to become independent and well-educated women, with Bachelors and even Master's degrees. She conducted Alcoholics Anonymous meetings and other drug and alcohol intervention counseling. She held Bible study every mandatory evening. Mrs. East would let you know about the God she served.

The name Phoebe came from the book of Romans when Jesus Christ acknowledged the help of a woman named Phoebe because she was a helper of many. Mrs. East founded the Phoebe House on biblical principles. Mrs. East was a licensed missionary after all, and her mission was to the needs of women in her city.

When Mrs. East finally called back, she said she could have had space for Mildred. I screamed in her ear my absolute thanks for her services and God! I knew she did some finagling to get her in. Mildred needed this breakthrough, and this was one of the best places. It was near the bus line, close to downtown, nearby doctor's offices, and the courthouse was just down the street. I could get to Mildred, and she could get to me. I was so excited that I could hardly sleep. I couldn't wait to get back to the hospital to give Mildred some good news for a change. I got up early the next morning with halleluiah on my mind. I had to shout, and tell God thank you! I took a shower and got dressed, and made it in time to catch the social worker who had made arrangements for the shelter in Enumclaw. I informed her that the Phoebe House had an opening for Mildred. I gave her their number so that she could call and make the arrangements.

RESTORE

Mildred had meanwhile gotten in touch with her sister in Maryland. Her sister was getting a ticket to come to Tacoma and get Ms. Olivia. There was only a week or so left before the eviction would become official. Things were finally moving! The optimistic look of Mildred's face was what I longed to see. She still had a long road to travel, and finally, she was walking forward.

The social worker completed the coordination of Mildred's discharge from the hospital to the *Phoebe House*. Mildred was extremely fearful, and her anxiety increased because she felt that John was going to be parked in a car somewhere, watching her leave the hospital. Mildred was going to wear a disguise when she left. She would not leave the hospital unless she was disguised. The police escorted her to the Phoebe House in the late evening, pulling her to the rear of the house. Mildred was finally in.

You can't imagine the relief I felt knowing she was safe. I went over to Mildred's house to check on her mother. I remembered driving around the block a few times to see if I was being followed. John was out there somewhere—I could feel it. I knocked on the door and Ms. Olivia opened it and let me in. I told her that Mildred was out of the hospital and in the *Phoebe House*. We sat down, and I told her everything about the Phoebe House, and that Mildred would be staying there for her protection. We weren't sure of John's whereabouts, but we knew he was out there somewhere. She told me that her daughter was coming and that she would be leaving to go stay with her. She needed support that Mildred could not give her at this time, yet she did not want to leave Mildred here, nor did she want to see her without the children. I asked her if she was fearful of being in the house, and that I would contact the police so that they could watch the house. She adamantly said no. Ms. Olivia just did not have that type of fear of evil. She had her God, and that was all she needed. She relied on Him. Her voice was so strong and confident. I believe the God in her life was the same God in my life, so I did not fear either. God did not give us the spirit of fear, but of love and a sound mind. Ms. Olivia's mind was sound!

I looked around the house and I looked in the refrigerator. She had a few things and wanted me to go to the store. She gave me a list along with some cash, and I went to the store to get the items. I was back in about 30 minutes with her things. I took the groceries out of the bag for her and put them on the table. I reached in my purse to give the cash she gave me back. She moved my hand, she would not take the money. I had paid for the food with my own money, and now she was making me keep hers. Ms. Olivia was strong-willed like that. You couldn't make her do anything she didn't want to do. I leaned over and hugged her. We stood there and just held each other for a few moments. I told her that I would check in with her and that Mildred would be giving her a call from the *Phoebe House* in the morning.

The next morning, I went straight to my office. I had not been in for two days. I checked my messages and returned some phone calls. I had already told some clients that I had a family emergency. The Phoebe House was one of my business clients. I had a contract with the Association to provide accounting services. I did the work there in their accounting office. I went later that afternoon. I went into Mrs. East's office to personally thank her. I also needed to inform her about some other things that pertained to Mildred and her mother. She had already spoken with Mildred and was aware of her elderly mother's situation. I told her that Ms. Olivia needed to see her daughter Mildred before she left and that she had not seen Mildred since the day the ambulance took her away from their home. Phoebe House had a 30-day 'block-out' policy during which participants are assessed. They did not allow outside contact with family and friends during this time. Mrs. East made the exception in this case because of the circumstances. She always was conscientious of her client's needs.

Next, I went into Doris's office. Doris was a short, light-skinned African American female case manager. She was a passionate woman when it came to Phoebe House clients. She had a beautiful smile. She enjoyed her job and would later be Mildred's case manager. She told me Mildred's room assignment, and I went upstairs to see how she was settling in. This was quite an environment for Mildred. She was in a shelter with women from various backgrounds. There were women there that had been abused, that were getting out of jails and prisons, women with alcohol and drug addictions. Here she was, a devout Muslim that did not drink, smoke, nor eat pork. She was surrounded by women with many societal dysfunctions and her insecurity probably stemmed from the feeling of doing nothing wrong but being married to a dangerous man. I reiterated to her that the Phoebe House was a clean and sober transitional home. All the women were trying to obtain some level of self-sufficiency either through school, legal help or in getting their children back. Some were getting visitation with their children because they were in the Phoebe House. All the women had some type of personal plan to get their lives back together, and I encouraged her to use the time at the Phoebe House to get healthy to figure out what she wanted to do. She needed to get the legal resources so that she could evaluate her situation properly. I explained that her mother would be able to visit her before she left to live with her sister. She was also going to allow some of the women to help her pack and get her things out of the home. Soon, Mildred's situation began to take on a new course of direction; a course of stabilization and empowerment. These were the first steps.

It had now been two weeks since Mildred had been at Phoebe House. I went over to Mildred's house to get her mother. When I arrived and greeted her, I could hear the excitement in Ms. Olivia's voice. She had been up most of the night baking sweets and making homemade candy to bring to Mildred. She was preparing to embrace and reassure her daughter, and like all mothers, the sweetness of the homemade pralines was meant to comfort. No matter how old one got, the relationship between mother and daughter remained. She did not waste any time gathering her things and flying out of the door with purpose and love. When we arrived I showed Ms. Olivia into the living room of the Phoebe House, and there she saw her daughter, waiting anxiously for our arrival. Their eyes lit up, and they embraced each other. She handed Mildred the bag of goodies, and Mildred and I shared them like two schoolgirls sharing in some kind of secret. Oh, they were good. I left them there to be alone. They had much to talk about.

I went back to the accounting office and did some much-needed work, and Mrs. East met me there to get a status on Mildred's mother and her living arrangement. She had already stopped by the living room and introduced herself to Ms. Olivia. I told her that Ms. Olivia was going to be leaving and that

RESTORE

Mildred's sister had purchased a ticket and would be here tomorrow. I asked again if the rules could change so that Mildred would be able to spend time with her mother and sister before they left. Mrs. East agreed to allow them whatever time they needed. I gave Mrs. East a big hug. I knew that she had helped many women like Mildred and worse. I now had firsthand experience of how valuable the *Phoebe House* was and for the first time, I was able to actualize the extent of resources I had for not only Mildred's case but other women as well.

Everything in Mildred's life had changed so suddenly, from being a successful businesswoman to now being in a shelter. Nothing would ever be the same. The blessing of the moment, however, yielded that she and her mother were out of immediate danger. Something that perhaps I or any other person would take for granted is our sense of security. I had spoken to Mildred's sister on the phone since Mildred had no direct phone line, and I discovered that her sister too was a Christian woman who had been praying fervently to the Lord for her sister, her nieces, nephew, and their mother. Often I would let Mildred use the phone in the accounting office to call her sister. I cautioned Mildred that no one could know that I was giving her these privileges. It could start serious contentions with her and other residents. When Mildred finally spoke directly to her sister, they did not hesitate and began making preparations to relocate their mother. I was looking forward to meeting Mildred's sister. Mildred and I both were looking forward to seeing Ms. Olivia in a safer and more secure place to live. Everyone, at that moment, was just waiting to exhale.

When her sister arrived, Mildred spent most of the day sharing the horrid details of the events that had taken place. Her sister arrived with her husband. Within 24 hours they were on their way back to Maryland. A week had gone by since Mildred's family had left Tacoma. Without her children, no husband, her mother gone, and now her sister, Mildred was by no doubt lonely. She now had no family in Tacoma, during perhaps her most vulnerable yet courageous of times. I was the only person that she knew in the Phoebe House the only one who she could trust. Our friendship turned more into family every day. Our friendship increased through bonds of devotion to each other. We shared almost everything.

The Phoebe House supported Mildred in a way that she had not experienced. The doors were locked from the outside in. No one could get in, but you could go out. That was how Mrs. East designed it. Women could leave the program whenever they wanted, and no one was forced to stay. Once you left, you would risk not getting back in. Your bed was usually given to the next person on the waiting list. Mildred was beginning to develop a rhythm. She was abiding by the Phoebe House guidelines. She was attending meetings and going to counseling. She was very polite to the women. She always replied "yes ma'am" and "no ma'am" to Mrs. East. She was doing her share of the work that had to be done in the home. She was preparing nutritional meals. She was a vegetarian and her meals were nutritious for everyone. In her quiet time alone she would pray and meditate. She listened to music by gospel artist Yolanda Adams titled "Open My Heart."

She had thirty days of "block-out," which was a critical component of the Phoebe House. Women needed to spend this time focusing on the matters before them. Mrs. East knew it would be easier for the women if they didn't have any distractions or any negative influences. Mildred needed this time for herself; it was the first time that she did not have the responsibilities for her mother. She had only the responsibility for herself.

She was looking well from the outside. She looked more rested and the glow in her eyes and smile was returning surely. She was now dressing in mainstream clothing that was provided by the Phoebe House. Mildred's case manager was Doris Berry. Doris and Mildred hit it off well. Doris was kind-hearted and very attentive to her clients. She was one of the kinds of people who are just right for social work. The patience that she had was incredible. Doris conducted Mildred's assessment. Mildred had access to many types of resources now.

Mildred applied for public assistance. The Phoebe House required every client to apply. If awarded, a percentage of the money went to pay for your room and meals. If you were not eligible, you still received services. She was eligible for General Assistance Unemployment through the Department of Social and Health Services. The most you could receive was $339 per month. It was more than she had, and it was coming inconsistently. She received food stamps that she contributed to the Phoebe House to help with the food. This is one of the ways communal living operates. The Phoebe House corroborated with many other non-profit and community-based organizations for services. One of the organizations was the YWCA. They had a shelter for women, legal assistance by attorneys, and case management. One of the things Mildred needed to do was figure out what her legal rights were.

After the 30-day 'block-out' period there was more flexibility with her schedule. She still had tremendous anxiety and fear of

John ending her life. How was she going to face this Goliath? According to the authorities, John had all the power. He was the children's biological father. Despite housing and caring for her children after the departure of John, despite surviving his threats and the toll they took on her health and well-being, despite her God-given right to be a mother, the authorities said John had rights, even if that meant they came at the expense of her rights. This seemed crazy to me. Why couldn't they find the children and let the family judicial system intervene? It doesn't matter if things had been vice versa; a parent shouldn't be able to just pick up the kids and disappear at the expense of the other parent. Each parent should be protected as should the children. With the types of threats that John had made, was he not a potential threat to his children? The children should be put into protective custody until the parents can get to court. A missing child is a missing child.

There was a detective from the Tacoma Police Department who had been working with Mildred from the beginning. The FBI was also contacted on grounds that John may have fled the country with the kids. Agent Shane from the FBI said that there was no proof of this, so they would not get involved. As the months went by, the relentless days gave Mildred more strength. The early months were difficult. Mildred continued to go outside disguised and would not wear the traditional Muslim headscarf. If John planned to destroy her, she wasn't going to make it easy. She stayed in the Phoebe House away from doors and windows. John had many friends and was the mechanic for most of the black people in the community. The word was out on the street that John had been asking people if they had seen Mildred. Mildred's new problem became how to be in the public, seek public services, and yet go under the radar of John's plot. The services that she needed required her to get out. She had appointments with therapists and doctors. She attended domestic violence and abuse meetings at the YWCA. Boldly and bravely, Mildred went out each day taking every precaution imaginable. When she would return, she would settle in and participate in the house activities. Mildred's smile and personality were contagious, and she began to make new friends at the Phoebe House. I was amazed at how the women began to imitate her in certain ways. Some of the ways were in hygiene. She explained to them a lot about the importance of proper undergarments and coverings. She did not force any of her Islamic beliefs on anyone; however, it sure did influence some. I saw women that didn't wear bras when they arrived at the Phoebe House wearing bras and camisoles. Even some of the toughest, abrasive females eventually succumbed to her genuine smile and kindness. Mildred was small in size compared to most of the women. I would tease Mildred about some of them. She said her strategy was not to join them but to make them her allies. Allies is what they became because the women had pulled together $200.00 of their own money to give to Mildred. She would hire a private investigator to try and find her children. Remember these are women with little money, living in a shelter, and transitional home with only each other and the kindness of the public. That was an act of love.

One day I was working in the accounting office when Mildred knocked on the door. She had been waiting for me, and as she entered she had a familiar look on her face, one that let me know she had a brilliant idea. She pulled out a piece of paper to show me. It was an advertisement for a paralegal home study course. She had clipped it out of a magazine. I read it and looked at her to see what she wanted me to do with it. She didn't understand why I wasn't excited. Sometimes I am so analytical that simple things are not noticed immediately. Mildred drew my attention to the cost of the course. It was only $5. I now knew why she was so ecstatic. The course included divorce, child custody, collections, and a variety of other information. All that for $5.00? It was neither a typo nor an error. It was indeed $5.00.

Mildred didn't have $5.00. All I had was $5.00, and I was hungry. It was my lunch money, but I gave it up. She walked out of the office grinning. Mildred had been volunteering at the YWCA in the legal department. It was a strategic move because she was working on her divorce from John. She was putting the proper pieces in place to get her children back, but this time she was going to use the law to her advantage. About three weeks had gone by since the $5.00 episode.

Mildred knocked on the office door and entered with a package. It was big and heavy. She had that familiar look on her face again. We opened the package and it was the paralegal course. What a course it was!. It had a lot of stuff in it for $5.00. There were books, manuals, tapes. It was a real home study course. I was in total shock that it only cost $5.00. GOD was in the blessing business, and this was a big one. When Mildred left the office she took her box and went straight to her room. She was like a child in a candy store. This was her new goodie bag.

Mildred was full of information. Mildred would speak with the attorneys at the YWCA that provided the pro bono work to its clients. She spoke with the law clerks and the court clerks. She would have them review drafts of her divorce filings. Mildred did not have a dime to her name, and she did everything by handwriting. When she would take her paperwork to the courthouse, a clerk would make corrections and Mildred would re-do the paperwork. Mildred was at the courthouse often speaking with whoever would give her information to assist her in the legal maze of filing for a divorce pro-se. The courthouse staff was so accustomed to seeing her that they began to empathize with her. Mildred would share with them her story. They even knew her by her first name. They were in support of her journey to find her children. Even the judges she appeared before wished her success in her journey to find her children.

She was filing her divorce papers, filing her child custody and parenting papers. She had to run an ad in the newspaper announcing her intent to divorce. This was how you file when you can't locate the spouse. She learned to write court pleadings. She went down to the county clerk's office and filed her papers. She filed a writ of habeas corpus, which was a document that mandated any law enforcement authority to pick up the children and extradite them to Tacoma if they were found.

After posting her divorce filing in the newspaper for the required amount of days in hopes that John would respond, the judge granted her divorce. Not only did they grant her the divorce, but also she was granted sole custody of her missing children. She was granted permission to leave the state. The dissolution of her marriage to John Allen Williams was the pivotal point of Mildred' turning from victim to victory in her previous spiral of defeat, victimization, and despair. She went from powerless to empowered with the legal papers to back her up.

Although Mildred had this victory, she still did not have her children. The only thing she could do was to wait it out. She had progressed into the transitional housing phase of the Phoebe House's program and was hired by the organization. Phoebe

House was staffed 24 hours a day. Mildred worked as the night staff member. Saving money was the goal.

InPowerMent (In Power Me) – MY REVELATION OF COURAGE

Mildred was known as Millie at the Phoebe House. She had been in the Phoebe House for about fifteen months. By then, she was being paid a stipend as Phoebe House staff. She worked the graveyard shift. This was a new position that was created at the Phoebe House as part of their employment readiness and on the job training program. Mildred was a good worker. Her administrative skills were very good, and the *Phoebe* House benefited from them. Mrs. East was proud of Mildred. She had grown fond of her over the months and watched another woman grow to become healthy and self-sufficient.

The only question was, where were her children?

It seemed as if the children had vanished. Mildred had been optimistic, and perhaps she was now accepting the reality that she needed to go be with her family on the east coast. She missed her mom. Everything that she could do, she had done. She was legally divorced and had sole custody of her children with permission to leave the state. Mildred was preparing to leave the last place where she saw her three children alive.

Everything was in order. She was not the same Mildred as before. She had more courage, more strength, and more determination to survive. She was going to be there when her children were returned. She was going to be well and ready to take them into her arms. Mildred spoke with Mrs. East about her plans to go back east to Maryland. Mrs. East supported her

RESTORE

decision. They developed an exit strategy that would get Mildred away from the Phoebe House, away from Tacoma, and away from Washington. The news of Mildred's departure spread throughout the Phoebe House. There was this stillness. Everyone wanted what was best for Mildred and wanted to witness the reuniting of her and her children. I was going to miss Mildred the most. I was going to miss my good friend. We had gone through some difficult times. I knew though that being with her family would be best for her. I wanted to go back to southern California myself to be with my family. I was going through some unhappy times. My marriage was cracking. Now I would not have any diversion from the issues I faced daily in my own home life. My abuse was not physical, it was psychological and emotional. My wounds were internal. I was hemorrhaging on the inside.

Mildred and I didn't discuss much of my perils. Over fifteen months what was going on in my life didn't feel paramount to what she was going through. My husband and I were not communicating, and he wasn't coming to our home at night. Silence and alienation were our way of getting through the *disease* within the marriage. There are many times I find myself outpouring into other's needs without considering my own. I am loyal when it comes to the few friends I have. I'm a giver first. I do expect to receive according to the measure that I'm giving. Somehow I come up with the short end of the stick. Mildred did not initiate conversations about me or mine. I had many concerns for myself and my children. I know how much she loved and missed her children. As a mother, I felt a tremendous void at the thought of someone just taking my children away. Although I was in constant turmoil that my marriage was becoming more and more irreconcilable. I was scared that I was going to be alone. So that I wouldn't have to face my trials, it was easier for me to dive into Mildred's life than to deal with my own life. I had spent the last fifteen months not even focusing on how I was feeling about my life. I was facing the reality that she was moving on to grab her future and somehow hold on to her past. My position as the accountant for the Phoebe House was not going to be the same without Mildred. Going there to work every day allowed us to comfort each other. We had some good times and we celebrated one another.

Mildred had made copies of all her court documents to leave with Mrs. East in the event there was ever any breakthrough and needed the proper documentation to get her children once they were found. She left the address and telephone numbers to her sister's home in Maryland. She was now officially ready to go. Mildred and I embraced for the last time. We had gone as far as we could to find her children. Our friendship was going to be long-distance. I encouraged her to remain brave. I believed that God was going to give us whatever we needed. It was going to be a matter of time before her children will be found and returned to her. Mildred left the Phoebe House and flew to Maryland. She telephoned me when she got settled to let me know that she had arrived safely. When I hung up the phone tears came to my eyes. I didn't cry, but they were there.

She continued to keep in touch with me. She kept her ears to the ground in Tacoma from Maryland. She informed me that she had found a job and was working. Her mother was no longer in Maryland but in Texas staying with her other sister, and she intended to visit them. According to Mildred, Ms. Olivia was fine. She was still the same, doing the same, but only in Texas.

RESTORE

We laughed — wasn't it interesting how life could sway people in so many directions, and yet somehow we all endured? Talking to Mildred got less frequent for the next few months. She was busy, and I was now in my income tax preparation season. My life at home was the same. I focused on my daughters. I had my oldest daughter going away to St. Augustine's University in Raleigh, North Carolina. My youngest was going into high school. I tried to focus on my marriage, but I remained in silent mode most of the time. I sensed a lack of mutual interest, but I tried to do whatever I could to make amends. It was just a one-way effort.

John Allen Muhammad Speaks – MY REVELATION OF HIS TRUTH

It was on a Saturday that I was lounging around the house when the telephone rang. When I said hello, a voice that I didn't recognize spoke.

"*Hello, Sistah.*"

I responded to the obscure yet familiar voice. "*Hello, who's calling please?*"

"*John,*" the man on the other end replied.

The shock of that name had me flipping through any Johns I had known.

"*John?*" I replied. "*John who?*"

He said "*John Muhammad.*"

I was almost mute. I did not expect to hear from him.

"*How are you, Sistah?*" he asked.

I told him I was doing well, although I was in shock! I asked how he was doing and how were the children. I told him Mildred had been looking for him for months. Everyone has been looking for him but had no way to reach him. I told him that Mildred had hired a private investigator to find him.

John laughed and said, "As you can see, I can be found if I want to be found. If I don't want to be found, no one is going to find me."

"Why did you disappear," I found the courage to ask.

John laughed and said the children are fine and that they were in school. He said they were active and taking swimming lessons. He said they were traveling and visiting places when they were not in school.

"Do you know where Mildred is?"

I instinctively told him I didn't have her address. I said she was frightened of him and did not leave any contact information. I told him that she would contact me by email, and that was how we stayed in touch. I asked if he had her email address and if he tried emailing her.

"You know I don't do the computer thing."

I asked if he had a telephone number that I could give to her. He gave me a cell phone number. I wrote it down. It had a 206 area code prefix. I asked if he was in Seattle or in our town somewhere. He said he was, and he would keep in touch with me. He kept asking me to have his *former* wife call him, the *former* unbeknownst to him. He said that they needed to talk and that the children missed their mother and wanted to talk to her. John said that he had to go and would call me back.

He told me that I had always been a righteous sister and a good friend to them. John's demeanor was calm and sincere. He spoke as if he had not done anything wrong. I wanted to get as much information about John as I could. I wanted to keep him in conversation. If I was not at the hospital that day when he called and threatened Mildred, I would have felt that he was compassionate and benign. I would have believed him.

As he spoke to me that day, I replayed the horror on his ex-wife's face from that day in the hospital. I will never forget the sound of her voice pleading to him to see her children—a mother much like myself, unable to embrace her own flesh and blood. John was once a smiling man, a man who had complimented me, now telling me I was his friend and expected me to fit into his scheme. This was a man who had caused his wife so much pain and yet here he was, as calm as a deer lying beside the still waters.

I emailed Mildred and told her that John had called me. In my message, I tried to capture every detail of our exchange. He was particularly irritated by a friend of Mildred's, Olivia, who was a sister and member of their mosque. I wrote:

Yes, Mildred he called the house. I had just come back from San Diego when I got the call. We spoke for about an hour. He said hello, may I speak to Isa. So, I asked who is calling. He said John. I said John who? He laughed and said John Muhammad. I said who? He said John Muhammad and then he asked how many John Muhammad's do you know? I said this isn't funny, who are you? You know John and Mildred! I said tell me something only you and I would know. He did and then he asked me where you were?

After I got over the initial shock, I had to calm myself to think what I should do and say. He stated that he needed to talk to you, that he hasn't seen you in over a year. YES, HE IS BITTER TOWARDS YOUR FRIEND, OLIVIA! He said he was on the run from place to place because Olivia had convinced you to call the police, the FBI, the Military Intelligence... He was calling me on a cell phone. He mentioned he was coming from Canada. (This may not be true.)

ISA FARRINGTON-NICHOLS

The only thing I wanted to do was to keep him talking, that's why I listened most of the time as he shared his version of the story. I mentioned that you had been sick, that your mom was in critical condition and living with other family members. He asked me if I had a number. I said no. Mildred, John seems to trust me. He feels that you and Olivia have "poisoned everyone's mind towards him." I asked him what I could do to help. He gave me Olivia's phone number; he wants me to call her and ask if she would tell me where you are. I led John to believe that if Olivia would contact you about me, maybe you would call me. (I told John I had not seen you in over a year.) John would not give me a number to contact; he said only that he would call me again. I asked him what his goal is if I should hear from you. He said talk to her sister! You are the only one whose mind is not poisoned. I know she will listen to you. That I have always been righteous by you and him. YES, HE STILL THINKS YOU ARE MARRIED. I then asked again...John what is your goal? Do you want to see her? How can I help? I told him you are probably right, in that she would confide in me. He said Talibah (sic) just turned eight and she wanted to talk to her mom for her birthday, but he couldn't find you. He said Selena has braces. He said Lil John's forehead is at his chin. I told John that you are probably still in the area, that you wouldn't leave the area without the children. He agreed. He repeated, "Just talk to her sister." Mildred I left a message with the private investigator again, right after I talked to John. I will call again tomorrow. MILDRED WE NEED A PLAN. Remember, I said you may have to come and face John if you want to see your children. I want him to think that I have reached you and were able to get you to talk to me. I want to talk to the investigator before I or we get back to him. As long as he thinks I can find you, he will stay in touch. Mildred, I will be praying for GOD's direction and guidance in this. I don't want to do my will, but GOD's will.

RESTORE

GOD is my defense and defender. I pray that GOD's HOLY SPIRIT will provide insight into all the mysteries. I must hear from GOD before I talk to John again. If John sees me as a righteous sister, then I can only attribute that as testimony of GOD's spirit within me. All I want is to have you reunited with your children. I or we are ready to do this!!! YOU HAVE THE LAW ON YOUR SIDE.

I LOVE YOU MILDRED.

Mildred didn't waste any time calling me back. She had so many questions. I didn't know where to begin. I told her again everything he said. I gave her the cell phone number that he had left with me. I asked her if she was prepared to come here to meet with him. Mildred was afraid to be with him because of the many threats to destroy her. She knew he was capable of carrying out his threats. I asked what she wanted me to do. She decided to give the information to the detective who had worked on her case.

The next day I received a call from the detective. He said that he was going to run a check on the cell phone. I don't know if he did it or not. I didn't have confidence in the Tacoma Police Department any longer when it came to Mildred Muhammad. Since the hospital scene, John was supposed to have had a warrant out for his arrest. When Mildred volunteered with the Human Rights Domestic Violence office, she discovered that John had been stopped at different times for speeding and the officer let him go. If there was a warrant in place, would the officer have let him go? We had no idea. When the officer stopped John, he certainly was not detained.

ISA FARRINGTON-NICHOLS

Trauma of my Drama – MY REVELATION OF HOPELESSNESS

Domestic abuse and domestic violence are so similar and yet so different. Abuse is deeply rooted with tentacles under the earth. You can have domestic abuse without the violence, but you cannot have domestic violence without the abuse. The abuse is the precipitation to the violence, whereas domestic violence is illegal. There is the physical manifestation of violence. It can be seen. Bruises are external and internal. They can be covered until healed—and perhaps then, there is still a slight mark that indicates the point of hurt.

Abuse is legal. Its bruises are internal with emotional and psychological damage. The wounds are deep and take longer to heal. Over time you are hemorrhaging on the inside. No one can see it. I would get up and adorn myself in my professional clothing. My nails were manicured, my feet had a pedicure. I lived in a nice house, drove a decent BMW, and I worshipped on Sundays. I was going through the mechanics of life, but on the inside, I was bruised and hemorrhaging from the trauma of my drama. I didn't recognize the extent of how I had drowned in this state until one day I woke up in the hospital from an emotional breakdown. I had stopped eating nutritional foods as my appetite diminished. I stopped socializing with close friends. I don't even remember getting any therapy at the time. I just let time be my Band-Aid.

The Tacoma community was desensitized to domestic abuse. Just looking at how Mildred pleaded and fought for the attention of our local, state, and federal agencies, the threats on her life were not even taken seriously. She told them that John was a demolition expert and was capable of violence. Because there were no signs of violence, they just documented her statements and filed them. John had not physically abused her. Mildred dressed nicely, had her hair done, and kept her nails manicured. No one could see the trauma from her drama.

When John would call I would always tell my husband, Joseph. Joseph would listen and ask if I was okay. We didn't think too much about it. My intention was truly to help Mildred get her children. It wasn't like we felt it was our responsibility, but we felt the authorities or the courts would handle it once they found John and the children.

John continued to call me from a 206 area code and repeat the same line:

"Isa, this is John, have you heard from Mildred?"

I reminded John of how fearful Mildred was of him. She believed he was going to destroy her. Mildred told me not to give him details of her whereabouts or happenings and to get whatever information I could from him about her children and his plans. This would all go to the detective. John would tell me the children were fine, and I'd relay this to the detective. He said that Lil' John was going to flight school to learn to fly airplanes, so I told this to the detective also. He stated that they were living in Canada, and I made sure the detective knew this. Salena and Taalibah were growing and going to school. John said he promised them that he would find their mother and unite them. I made sure the detective knew John's supposed intentions.

I told John that I had emailed Mildred, but that I had not received a response. I did email Mildred, and she was not trying to be caught alone with John. She felt that he was going to destroy her. I told John that Mildred and her mother had left Tacoma. I never told him where. I asked if he knew where her relatives lived and he replied no. John did not call in a few months. Maybe I watch too much crime drama on television. I just knew that the police department had sophisticated technology. I just knew they were going to track him through the cell phone, but the 206 area code didn't reveal anything to the detective.

I could only wonder if Mildred were white, would it have made a difference how everyone treated this case? Could all of this trauma be prevented if the initial trauma in the home had been heeded and addressed? This trauma began in one home and would later seep into so many lives. I feel that Mildred's case was given little priority. The shame of this lack of action, lack of attentiveness, lack of absolute concern for her welfare, would haunt Tacoma and the nation forever. At that time, it was unimaginable what John was capable of, and instead, Mildred's case was treated as just another case of marital woes.

Who would have imagined Tacoma's own police Chief David Brame, killing his wife and himself in front of their two children? Chief Brame used his position to stalk and terrorize his wife. Here we are talking to Chief Brame, the same *"Chief Brame"* whose very own wife put a restraining order against him and moved. We were expecting to get support for Mildred and the abduction of her children, while Chief Brame was seemingly disinterested and told us that they heard about a thousand cases like this per day. Who would imagine he was one of these cases? Who would have imagined a decorated police chief like Brame, or an army veteran, a family man, a person heralded in his community, such as the infamous John Allen Muhammad, being capable of recruiting a child accomplice to terrorize the nation's capital, numerous states, and the entire nation? The one thing in common in both cases is that both men were abusing their wives!

It was a beautiful day in Tacoma. We had our entire family over for a barbecue. The Nichols family enjoyed barbecues and parties. We would make up any reason to have one. My husband was an excellent grill man. He would marinate ribs, chicken, and hot links in his marinade sauce overnight. He would get up early at 7:00 AM and start preparing the barbecue grill on the patio. I would get up around 9:00 AM and start with the side dishes. I would prepare appetizers of divine eggs (I changed the name from deviled eggs), vegetable trays, and cheese and cracker trays. I would then start boiling some ham hocks for the greens. I would make my popular *Isa Beans* and put the potatoes on for potato salad. We would then go and groom ourselves. By 2:00 pm we were ready for guests to arrive at 3:00 pm. It was like clockwork. That very day, I got one more call from John using the same cell phone number. He said he wanted to check in with me, and he wanted to know if Mildred had replied to my email. He said he was in the Bellevue, Washington area. Bellevue is about a 45-minute car ride from Tacoma. I asked him about the children. This time he did not tell me anything about his children. He ignored the question as if I hadn't asked. I didn't repeat the question. I just felt it was strange. I told John that I had to go because I had company. We hung up and I went back outside to tell my husband that John called. Joseph asked me what he wanted and I told him that it was the same questions about Mildred's whereabouts.

"Did you give him her number?"
"No, Mildred doesn't want him to have it."

ISA FARRINGTON-NICHOLS

The doorbell rang. I assumed it was more guests. I looked out the window, and standing there with a wrinkled green suit, dark-colored shirt, white athletic socks, and old brown penny loafer shoes was a tired-looking man. He looked as though he had just crawled out of a bed with his clothes on.

I opened the door. There were no children. There were no answers. I had not seen John in about two years. And yet, he smiled.

"How you doing, Sistah?"

You can't get to my house in Tacoma from Bellevue, Washington in fifteen minutes. I uttered that I was well and just stared at him, his eerie persona there at the door of my home, unable to hear anything he was saying.

I remember looking into his eyes, the noise gone, the smell of barbecue no longer present. Those eyes that had looked so endearingly upon Mildred were now the eyes of wrath and destruction. I did not want to lose myself in those monstrous eyes. I crawled out of my thoughts and remembered my manners. My guests were starting to arrive, and I invited him inside. I wanted Joseph to see him, to see the being that stood before me. John followed me to the deck where the family was and greeted them. He even hugged my mother-in-law. We all were surprised by his unannounced visit. We decided not to mention anything about Mildred and his children. In our home stood a man who threatened a harmless woman, a man who abducted children, a man who was determined to ruin lives. This being was in my home. He was mingling with our guests. We did not know what to expect from him. We said nothing.

RESTORE

Joseph offered John a plate of food. He fixed him some BBQ chicken, greens, beans, and potato salad. I mentioned that my famous *Isa Beans* had pork, but John ate it anyway. Muslims do not eat pork. It is forbidden. Joseph and I looked at each other as he ate all the food on his plate. He ate as if he had not had a meal in a while. When John finished eating we walked to the front porch.

John began to talk about what led him to take his children. He had been separated, but he wanted to work things out. He said that he and Mildred had argued and separated before but would always consider their need for family. Then they would work things out between them. He said that Mildred was being influenced by her friend from the mosque, Olivia, and felt that Olivia was influencing Mildred to challenge her husband. This was the first time that he and Mildred were not able to work things out on their own because of Olivia's strong influence over Mildred. John believed that if he could just talk to Mildred that she would come back. He just needed to talk to his wife the way they had done in the past. John wanted me to tell Mildred that they could work things out. I asked John why he took the children. John used a metaphor of a burning house. He said that Mildred was having telephone conversations with a man that she met over the internet. He said he found out by recording their telephone conversation. He said that all he could do was wonder if she had lost her mind. He felt that she could be talking to a pedophile and not know it. He felt that she was putting his children in danger. When he approached her about it she didn't care.

John felt that it was like his house was burning, and when your house is burning you don't ask why or any questions. You just get your loved ones out. You find out later what caused the fire. John said that his wife's behavior with the man she met on the internet was dangerous. It was fire, and he wasn't going to stand by and wait for something to happen to his children. So he took them. Now he was ready to talk to Mildred because apparently, the fire was out. I've heard the adage: two sides to a story. This conversation was an entirely different side of the story.

I stood there looking into John's eyes. I didn't know what to do with the conversation. I had no response. Joseph joined us on the front porch, and we walked John to his car. John noticed that we had a white Nissan 300ZX parked in the driveway. He said that he thought it was his car. John and Mildred owned a white Nissan 300ZX with a burgundy interior. He walked carefully around the car. He noticed the only difference was that their car had leather seats, and this one in the driveway had fabric.

Joseph and I stood there while he studied the car. Now we knew why he stopped by. He saw the car and thought Mildred was at our house. The Nissan 300ZX was too coincidental. He had to stop. Joseph and I did not even own this car. It was on loan to Joseph from a friend of his. We had been driving the car for a couple of months. Both of our vehicles were inoperable at the time, and this was our only mode of transportation. I had not met Joseph's "friend" who owned this car. All I knew was that this friend's name was Sean. I assumed that Sean was a guy. It wasn't until later that I found out Sean was a female. I had been driving some woman's car for months.

John left our home and thanked us for the food. He encouraged us to help him find Mildred. He said he just wanted to talk to her, that his children missed her, and wanted to talk to

RESTORE

their mother. He promised them he would find her. I told him when she would contact me I would tell her what he said. He said the cell phone number was still the same.

I told John that the police were still looking for him and the children. His reply was not one of worry. His response was very casual.

"You know now; I will be found when I want to be found. If I don't want to be found, I won't be."

John was driving a brown car. I had someone write down the license plate number.

I emailed Mildred and told her about the unexpected drive. I told her verbatim what had happened. I told her that she needed to make some decisions. I asked if she was prepared to face John. She was going to have to face him if she wanted to see her children. Mildred's feelings were that of fear. She did not and could not trust John. She felt he was going to trap her and try to harm her. In her response, Mildred said she would not face John alone. She felt she would face him only with police protection, and even then she was not confident in the police.

Mildred took the information and contacted the Tacoma Police Department. She contacted the detective that was assigned to her. She gave them all the information I had given her. The detective ran the license plate number for the car that John showed up in. The car belonged to Rebecca Beeler in Olympia, Washington. For the first time, the police had a physical location to seek John. had eluded the police. I knew Rebecca and her husband They owned *Your Fish House*, a neighborhood eatery They were once clients of mine. They owned the few years and eventually sold it to someone e

ISA FARRINGTON-NICHOLS

Nation of Islam followers and worshipped at the same mosque with John and Mildred.

Mildred phoned me and said that the detectives were going to stake out the location of the address and see if the children were there. Becky and Walter knew where John was all along, and she recounted how she had asked them to help her, to call her if they heard anything. She left them with information to get a hold of her.

She provided the authorities pictures of her children, yet Mildred's hope was diminished when the detectives went to the address and only saw little children playing, who were gathered into the home by a woman who saw authorities approaching the home. They did not know if the children were hers or not. They had not seen John Muhammad.

Mildred and I remained in touch occasionally. Things were pretty cold on finding the children. The police had not done very much. They were swamped with other cases. They had very little to do with Mildred and her missing children. I never gave up praying for their safety and their return.

East Coast Bound - MY REVELATION OF COURAGE

working in my office one day when Mrs. East buzzed
down to her office immediately. The tone in her
in ious. She demanded that I stop whatever I was
to her office quickly. My heart throbbed. At
intense situations would occur. Whatever it
ne. What was the urgency I was hearing

RESTORE

I sat down in a chair in front of Mrs. East's desk. She closed the door silently, and with her action, she set a serious, almost dreadful air in the room. I just stared at her looking for some sign. She sat at her desk and played a message back over the speakerphone from the telephone. It was a call from someone in Bellingham, Washington's Department of Social and Health Services. They were inquiring about Mildred Muhammad.

I was confused. Mrs. East said that they were inquiring because a John Muhammad was applying for state aid for him and the children. When John applied, the children's names were already in their system. From this, it became clear that they had been listed already by Mildred when she was staying at *Phoebe House*. And she listed its location and number as her address, which prompted the social worker from Bellingham to inquire.

One of *Phoebe House*'s policies for its beneficiaries is that they must apply for state assistance. If they qualified, then a portion of their income would be used to help pay for their room and board. Mildred had applied in Tacoma, and she had listed her children on the application. Mrs. East told the social worker that those children were the missing children that had been abducted by their father.

When the social worker in Bellingham called back, she had contacted the Bellingham Police Department. She told us that someone from the Child Protective Services Department would be calling us and that this was now going to be handled by her supervisor. Mrs. East and I thanked her. Little did this social worker know that she was about to unlock the chamber of horror for a grandmother, a mother, and a family that had been traumatized by John's decision to abduct his children.

ISA FARRINGTON-NICHOLS

We were so hopeful that these were Mildred's children for whom John had potentially tried to solicit aid. Yet we did not know how this was going to play out. Mrs. East and I held hands, and we started praying. Praying was our routine at *Phoebe House*. It was a house of prayer. We had to pray for funding, for the resources needed for the women, and often for the operations of the center. We prayed for Mildred. We prayed for the safety of her children. We prayed that God would restore these children to Mildred. We called on our Savior, Lord Jesus Christ, to restore, redeem, and deliver these children from any further hurt, harm, and danger. We canceled, in the name of Jesus, any assignments that would stop these children from being traumatized any longer. The longer we prayed, the louder we prayed. We would take turns speaking to God calling on Him to intervene.

I was exhausted, but I kept praying. I kneeled to the floor and continued to pray, speaking the words in the scriptures that would pierce through principalities and spiritual wickedness in high places. Mrs. East began praying in the spirit with the Holy language of tongues. We both were speaking in tongues. An entire hour had gone by. We prayed until that phone rang, and like church bells, the ringing was that reminder of something sacred. It was the detective from children's services! The detective needed information about the children. We faxed him copies of Mildred's court documents and Mildred's telephone number in Maryland. We even gave the website address that Mildred had put on the internet. The website had pictures of the children on it. Mildred had developed this website in hopes that someone would have information on the whereabouts of her missing children. The detective said that he would give us a callback.

RESTORE

Mrs. East called Mildred and told her about the telephone calls. She gave her the name of the detective for her to call. We were hopeful. Mildred had been praying for this day. I will never forget the melodic tone of hope in her voice. Mrs. East asked Mildred when and how she was going to get back here to Tacoma. Mildred had a friend that worked at a travel agency, who knew of Mildred's story and who had told Mildred that she would be able to get her a flight to Tacoma when and if she needed one. Mildred was preparing to see her children John, Salena, and Taalibah. What did they look like? How had they changed? How would they receive their mother?

The Detective telephoned back the next day. He had spoken with Mildred and he was pretty sure that these were her children. They were going to the address that John gave on the application. The detectives had told the social worker to continue to process the aid application. They did not want John to get suspicious. The address that John had given was to a shelter in Bellingham, Washington. When the detectives arrived John and the children were not there. The shelter director identified the children from a picture; however, they were using different names. He said that John was working and the children were attending a nearby school.

The detectives arrived at the elementary school, and they spoke with the school's administrator. The administrator identified the children from the picture and stated they were enrolled and were in their classrooms. Again they were under different names. The detective explained that the children had been abducted. The school administrator went to have the three children taken out of class and brought to the office. One by one the children were brought into the office. It was over. Mildred's missing children were taken into protective custody. They were immediately extradited.

Mildred received a telephone call from the detective. This was one of those true moments when everyone's work profoundly brings rewards. For the first time in eighteen months, Mildred heard her children call her "mommy." That evening Mildred was on a flight to Tacoma, Washington. The travel agency came through with the ticket. She was arriving in Tacoma in the morning. Mildred would be reunited with her children.

I received a call from Mildred early in the morning. She was here in Tacoma at the YWCA where she used to volunteer. The sound of joy emanated from her, and the eagerness of being reunited with her three children, John, Salena, and Taalibah, was heavy in her voice. We both could hardly contain our emotions. Was it really over? Was this season of mayhem finally over? Had God delivered us from this particular evil? The confirmation would come at 9:00 a.m. when Mildred would be in court. Mildred asked me if I would come to the courtroom with her. Without any hesitation, I said that I would. It was a full circle. I had been with Mildred since the first day her children were taken by their dad. Now, I would be there when she would be reunited with them.

Eighteen Month Reunion – MY REVELATION OF THE COST I PAID

I arrived at the Tacoma Municipal Court House at about 8:30 a.m. I planned to be there to support Mildred and to welcome her children. It was not my intention to see a family torn apart. I have always felt that the court would decide what was equitable regarding custodial issues for both John and Mildred. Now that the children were in protective custody, the court would establish a plan for the children. The upbringing of children must never be at the decision or whims of just one parent. This was a vital and critical moment of intervention and prevention of lawful or unlawful children abductions.

When I cleared the security checkpoint, I saw Mildred in the foyer area. Our eyes locked and there was her beautiful smile. We embraced each other for a while. Mildred was trembling. I thought it was due to the emotion of being reunited with the children. Across the hall on a payphone was John Muhammad. He was staring at Mildred and I looked at him to acknowledge him. He just gave a cold stare that was not at me but Mildred.

Mildred ran. Her attorney caught her and immediately had her taken to the sheriff's office to wait until it was time for court. We found out that Mildred's court appearance was changed to 11:00 A.M. Anxiety overcame Mildred and the fear she felt in John's presence was emulated in that violent tremble that no courthouse or guards could cure. I too began to get nervous.

Around 10:45 A.M. we were escorted into the courtroom, where another case was in session. When we walked into the court, John was sitting in a seat. We had to take a seat and wait for their case to be heard. To accommodate Mildred, the attorney arranged for us to sit in the front so that Mildred did not have to look at John. Mildred reached over and grabbed my hand until the Judge called, "Mildred Muhammad vs. John Allen Muhammad."

Mildred and her attorney approached the judge. John approached the judge. He did not have an attorney. The judge looked over Mildred's file, which contained divorce papers and child custody papers. The judge carefully examined the documents in the court file. He commented how everything was in order. There were no errors or omissions. Mildred had filed for her divorce without the assistance of an attorney.

The judge looked at John and asked him if he had any questions.

"Your honor, why am I here?"

John wanted the judge to explain to him why his children were being taken from him.

The judge told John, "Mr. Muhammad, we are here to address the information in these documents."

John wanted to tell the judge his side of the story, but the judge would not allow him to address anything. It was not the purpose of the hearing. He told John he would have to get an attorney and schedule another court date. At that time, he would be able to address any of his concerns. This hearing was only to address the divorce and the returning of the children to the custody of their mother. The judge ruled in favor of Mildred Muhammad and ordered that the children be released immediately to Mildred Muhammad. John stood there looking perplexed.

John could only simply say, "So, don't get to see my children?"

From the moment the judge hit his gavel with a loud crack, his decision was rendered. Mildred was now about to see her three children. Eighteen months had gone by since she had seen them. It had been eighteen months since the day she took them to school and they did not come home. Mildred turned to me as I left my seat to join her. We held each other. We cried with joy. John had left the courtroom. He never said a word. Within minutes Mildred's attorney was calling child protective services informing them of the judge's decision, that Mildred would be coming to pick up her children. While standing in the hall outside of the courtroom, I stood along the wall. I looked at Mildred and her eyes bucked out. She dropped everything in her hands and started running down the court hallway corridor. She just took off. I didn't see anything. I wondered where she was going. The attorney ran down the hall after her. I still didn't see anything. As I began to follow them both, John walked right past me. He was walking rapidly toward Mildred. The look on his face was that of an angry man. I didn't know if he saw me or not.

 John turned around and walked right past me again. I stared at him as he walked by. He didn't say anything to me or even acknowledge my presence. I turned and ran down the hall corridor to join Mildred. When I caught up with them, Mildred and I were escorted and taken through a back corridor to exit the courthouse. When we came to the door there was a taxi cab waiting. We entered the taxi cab to take us to meet up with the children. I asked the cab driver to take me to my parked car. I felt that I needed to get my car and meet up with Mildred. The attorney told the cab driver to drive around several different blocks before taking me to my car. After what we just experienced at the courthouse she wanted to make sure that John was not following us. I didn't feel as if I was in any danger. Yet, I was going to be cautious. John knew where I lived. I felt he may come over to the house thinking that Mildred and the children would be there.

 When I arrived at the Department of Social and Health Services, Mildred and her attorney were standing outside in the parking lot. I parked my car and joined them during this extremely emotional moment. We waited for the children to be brought down to their mother. I wondered what they would say to one another. Had they grown much? Mildred and I had talked about this moment a long time ago. Now that day had come. Suddenly the door opened, and proclamations of Mildred's motherhood came pouring out of her children's mouths.

"Mommy! Mommy!" Taalibah and Salena sang out.

The girls ran to their mother. Mildred scooped them into her arms and cried and smiled. They held each other. I was cemented to the floor and couldn't move my feet. My eyes watered at the sight of the love that was so pure. The love and bond between mother and child. Lil' John came out of the office last. The children had grown so tall. They did not look like the children in their pictures that we posted everywhere. When they came out of the office the girls were in pants. Their hair was not combed. They had on clothes that didn't fit. They were un-kept and looked neglected. They looked like children that lived on the streets. They looked like transients.

Lil' John's hair was long. His clothes were old and dirty. He walked slowly to his mother. While the girls were happy, Lil' John had signs of resentment. He walked out with his hands in his pockets. She grabbed him and hugged him but he was stiff with anger, dirty clothes, and at the dawn of his teenage years.

"Hello, son," Mildred said.

She held him in her arms, and he looked apprehensive. He didn't hold his mother as his sisters had. He was reserved. I knew that he felt betrayed in some way. There was no telling what he had been told. He was standing there looking confused and protective of his little sisters. As Mildred and her children got into the cab to leave, I told her to call me when they got settled.

RESTORE

I went back home to check on my daughter, Tamara. I also called my husband Joseph. I shared with him the entire story. Joseph wanted me to go home in case John would come to the house. He did not want Tamara to be at home alone if he appeared. The very same thought had crossed my mind. When Tamara arrived home, I told her that Mildred finally had her children, and she asked if we could go see the children, and ensure that they were okay. Tamara wanted me to share every detail. I told her some parts, but not all of what happened. I wanted her to witness the answer to many prayers. I wanted her to witness how God is real and that we can depend on Him to deliver us from turbulent times. We talked about how good God had been to restore the children safely back to their mother.

Mildred and the children had gone to the Tacoma YWCA. When Tamara and I arrived, the children had been bathed. Mildred had selected some clean clothes from the Y's clothing closet. The girls were now in nice dresses. Mildred had washed and combed their hair. Lil' John was dressed in some nice pants and a shirt. His entire disposition had changed. He was smiling and they were glad to see us. I told Tamara to go hang out with the children. I wanted to talk to Mildred.

Mildred explained how she had shown the children the website and had explained her efforts in finding them. The children were really impressed with the website. It changed Lil' John's countenance towards his mother. He could see that she did try to find them. They had been told that she did not want them anymore and that she didn't love their family. While getting them cleaned up she answered their questions. She was resourceful and showed her children what she had done in their absence. She told them that she didn't ever stop searching for them.

The children coming back home to their mother was the first manifestation of restoration after much sacrifice. We had prepared Mildred for restoration, and she was finally reaping it. She communicated with them in the same instinctive way a mother does with her children. Mildred said that they were leaving on a red-eye flight that evening. The YMCA had gathered together funds for her and the children, and they were heading out in a taxi to the airport. I gave her some spending money and asked Mildred if she had spoken with Mrs. East from the *Phoebe House*. She said she had meant to contact her because she wanted Mrs. East to meet her children. I decided to give Mrs. East a call. When Mrs. East answered her phone, I told her I was at the YWCA with Mildred. I asked her if she would give them a ride to the airport that evening so that she could also meet Mildred's children. Without any hesitation, she said she would give them a ride. I took Tamara back home and told my husband that Mrs. East and I were going to take Mildred and her children to the airport. Mrs. East arrived at 9:00 p.m. to pick me up. We then drove to the YWCA to get Mildred and the children. The YWCA staff was taking all the necessary precautions for Mildred's safety. They had arranged for her to leave from a private entryway. Mrs. East and I pulled around to it and waited patiently for them to come out. Mrs. East hadn't considered the fact that John could be around following us until now. We had not considered that we could be in any kind of danger. What would we do if John showed up? A door opened and out came Mildred and the children. They entered into Mrs. East's Cadillac. With apprehension, we quickly drove away. Mildred introduced each one of her children to Mrs.

East, who commented on how beautiful and intelligent they were. She told them that their mother loved them, and she told them to take care of their mother.

They replied with that typical, polite, *"Yes ma'am."*

The conversation that we had in the car with the children rendered some answers to some questions. The children had shared some of their experiences. Taalibah shared a story of how she got into trouble because she had called her sister by her name Salena. They were not supposed to say their names any longer. She explained how her daddy got real mad when she called her sister Salena. Mrs. East marveled how bright and intelligent the children were. She hoped that Mildred would get them into counseling real soon. She had witnessed many times before, homeless and abused women being reunited with their children. This was another *Phoebe House* success story. Mrs. East had seen the results of another woman that came out of brokenness to being healed, delivered, and set free. It was for this reason that God had called Mrs. East to be a missionary and to establish the *Phoebe Houses*.

When we arrived at the airport we went to the ticket counter. The YWCA had made arrangements for them to get with the airport police. When airport security arrived, they escorted Mildred and the children to a waiting lounge until it was time to board the plane. I stood in the middle of the airport and waved as they walked down the airport corridor with airport police. Afterward, Mrs. East and I drove back to Tacoma.

CHAPTER 3

Let There Be Light!

"Therefore whatsoever ye have spoken in darkness shall be heard in the light; and that which ye have spoken in the ear in closets shall be proclaimed upon the housetops."
~ Luke 12:3

The First Tragedy and Untold Story – REVELATION OF MY HEART FOR FAMILY

Keenya, my niece was getting her life back on track. Keenya worked very hard on her job as a retail assistant manager at a women's clothing store. Keenya had moved in with her uncle Joseph Nichols, my husband so that she could get away from her physically and verbally abusive relationship with her daughter's father. She was a young single mother working hard to make ends meet. We met with her previously over dinner to discuss her goals, what she envisioned to be her accomplishments in life and to see if we could help facilitate. We agreed that Keenya's goals were obtainable and allowed Keenya to move into our home with the baby.

She later left her job to go on maternity leave, and then after giving birth she decided to go back to school. Keenya was applying for housing assistance, and she was completing all the tedious paperwork for various types of financial aid available to low-income, single mothers. Her interests were in restaurant management. She liked to cook, and she could cook well. Aside from all this, Keenya was a new mom and taking care of Angeleah, her baby girl. Angeleah was what she enjoyed most of all.

To be able to watch Keenya within the safety of our home and grow into the best mother was truly rewarding. She was willing to make whatever change she needed so that her baby would have a better quality of life. I watched her proceed with her life, making the necessary changes in her life to start being independent and to heal her feelings from abuse and neglect. She moving forward in replacing toxic feelings with love, high self-esteem, and education. Our decision to allow her and the baby to stay in our home meant that we were allowing God to use our blessings to bless her, to bless them. That's what Keenya was to me, a blessing.

The morning of February 16, 2002, I remember waking up to the telephone's ringing. It was my husband telling me that he and his brother had arrived safely in California. They were on their way to a friend's house, and I can recall telling Joseph to call me when he got settled.

"Okay," he said.

"I love you, and be safe."

"I love you too," he replied.

I laid back down because I had made up my mind that I was going to take some time to sleep in and just get the rest that my body needed. Once I knew Joseph was safe in California, and that everybody else was out doing their thing, I laid in bed until around 1:30 pm. After that good rest, I got up, made myself a nice hot cup of coffee, and made a couple of telephone calls. It was tax season and my business was preparing taxes for clients from my home office. One of my clients came over for their annual appointment. Most of my clients had been so for years, so our professional relationships automatically turned into friendships very easily. By having my practice at my home, the environment was much friendlier. I could offer my clients a beverage or a snack while I went through their tax information. It was also great because my male clients could watch sports on the television, while their wives would be doing the tax work with me.

At about 3:00 P.M., shortly after my clients left my home, Keenya arrived with the baby, and we decided to go to the grocery store. One of the agreements that we had with Keenya is that she would buy food as her contribution to the household. We didn't charge Keenya any rent or utilities. She would just contribute groceries. On this particular day Keenya, the baby, and I went to the *Safeway* grocery store. The baby was catching all the attention of everybody that walked by our cart. The baby was cooing, laughing at people, and giving them big smiles. What would normally take 30 minutes to shop turned into an hour and a half because of all the attention the baby received. We also stopped to get something to drink on the way home. There, Keenya and I began to dialogue. Keenya shared with me how she had a wonderful weekend with the baby's father. It was Valentine's Day, and he had given her a flower and some Mylar

RESTORE

balloons. They got along that weekend, and she was feeling good about that. I was silent because I wanted to just listen as she shared with me. I wanted to keep my opinion and judgment to myself. I began to shift the conversation to our living arrangement and our agreement. I wanted to check in with her to see how she was doing with her goals, finances, and budget. I just wanted to make sure that she was still on task with what she wanted to accomplish and to see if there was anything she needed from me that would be helpful. We talked about our arrangement and how it was allowing her to save her money so that when the time came that she would get an apartment, she would be able to furnish it and have money for utilities, etc. There was just a very warm feeling in my heart as she explained to me what she had accomplished. We drove back home and brought the groceries into the house. Keenya asked me if I would fix some chicken tacos. Chicken tacos are a very popular meal and a favorite that I often would cook for my family. It was the request from them at least once a week. I told Keenya, sure, I would cook, but as we were putting up the groceries, I noticed we hadn't bought any taco shells. I told Keenya I would go back to the store later and get some taco shells. We put up the groceries, and I went back to working at my tax business. Keenya went upstairs to begin changing her baby.

I remember the doorbell ringing. Keenya's mom and her best friend came by. They were on their way to attend the Bill Cosby show. Keenya's mother was an avid Bill Cosby fanatic. She had wanted to attend the concert, and no one wanted to go with her. Finally, her best friend had purchased some tickets, and they were dressed up, going to have dinner, and see Mr. Bill Cosby. Keenya laughed. Her mother looked incredible that day. She just flounced around to every mirror in the house with her new outfit. She was so happy. She wanted to borrow binoculars to see the show. She wasn't sure where her seating would be and didn't want to miss anything. Keenya complimented how beautiful her mother looked. She kissed her mom and told her to have fun at the concert. Her mother went whisking out the door, looking glamorous. That was her nickname to most of her nieces and nephews—Auntie Glamorous.

Shortly thereafter the telephone rang and it was my 14- year-old daughter Tamara. Keenya had answered the phone and told her that we were going to make chicken tacos for dinner. Tamara insisted that we not make the chicken tacos since she was not home. Tamara was supposed to be at a sleepover, and all of a sudden, she told Keenya to tell me to pick her up. All of a sudden she had changed her mind about the sleepover, and she wanted to come home. I told Keenya to tell her that I would pick her up on my way to the store to pick up the taco shells and to be ready because I was going to honk the car horn. I grabbed my keys and left shortly thereafter. I remember vividly the order of events.

I walked out and closed the door. Then I went back into the house to tell Keenya to go into the freezer to get the frozen chicken breasts out and boil them so that when I returned, the meat would be ready.

She said, "Okay, Auntie."

Then I left, closing and locking the door again. I got in the car and commenced to go pick up Tamara. Afterward, I stopped at Safeway for the taco shells. For some reason, on the ride back home, I remembered that I needed to get some information from a friend about s softball tournament in February in Las Vegas. I had played with this co-ed softball tournament team for a few years and so this was on my mind going back home. The weather was a bit cloudy, and it was almost dark. Tamara and I were driving up the street towards our house. We pulled into the driveway. I told Tamara to go into the house and open the garage door because I was going to put the car into the garage for the evening. I sat there, listening to the local jazz station. What was taking Tamara so long to open the garage door? Tamara can be easily distracted, I thought. I began to get a little anxious because she should have had the door open by then. I looked up and Tamara had come back out to the car. She stood there with the most disarming look of shock on her face. As I stared at her, I could see something was wrong with my child. I got out of the car and I asked,

"Tamara, what is it? Why haven't you opened the door?"

She just stared at me. I kept asking, "Tamara, what is it?"

As I got out of the car to come close to her, she finally spoke.

"The house is all smoky and Keenya is lying on the floor."

I turned off the engine, took the keys out, and went to the front door. I saw Keenya lying in the doorway, with her feet at the front door and the rest of her body lying in the foyer of the house. As I looked into the house, there was a pot on the stove. The electric coil burner on the stove was orange. The smoke was at the top of the house. You could feel the heat from the kitchen from the stove burning. My first thought was that Keenya had succumbed to smoke inhalation. I ran into the kitchen and was able to get the stove turned off. I tried to remove the pot but it had melted onto the burner of the stove. I went back to Keenya. I kneeled over her body and grabbed her hand. I called out her name repeatedly. Keenya's eyes were open, glared, and fixed. They were just a blank, glazed stare. Her hands were cold and stiff. There was a small hole in her face, under her eye on the cheek.

I saw a small casing, a little metal casing next to Keenya's head, and I realized this was not smoke inhalation. I saw the little metal piece, but I didn't touch it. I immediately ran to the phone to dial 911. I was praying so hard. I felt so helpless.

I cried out, *"Lord, Lord Jesus, help us!"*

I prayed that Keenya would hang on.

I remember screaming to her, *"Hang on, hang on Keenya! Keenya, Auntie is here!"*

Within minutes after talking to the operator, I could hear sirens far off into the distance. The thought of Angeleah crossed my mind. I ran upstairs because I thought that the smoke might have affected the baby. I was so very fearful because the baby was lying on her stomach and was not moving. I didn't know whether or not if something had happened to the baby. So I touched her back, and she jumped up and started screaming and crying. The baby was naked and had rolled her way to the edge of the bed. Near the bed, there was a change of pajamas, fresh unused diaper, and bottle of warm milk. As I grabbed Angeleah and held her, the baby just grabbed my shirt, screaming and yelling. I grabbed the towel, the blanket, and wrapped the baby up, and she began to calm down. I did not know how long the baby had been lying there, but apparently, she had cried herself to sleep when her mom had not returned.

I came downstairs. I handed the baby to Tamara who was standing on the front porch in the same position she was in when I left her. Tamara was in shock. She had not moved the

RESTORE

whole time. She would not come into the house. She could not speak. I handed her the baby on the front porch to hold. It never occurred to me that someone could still be in the house, but I could still hear sirens coming closer. I turned to Tamara, and I told her to take the baby and go to our neighbor's house. Tamara left with the baby. I told her to go and call her grandmother.

Finally, the paramedics arrived, and the fire department arrived too. They came in, and they saw Keenya lying there. They pulled Keenya from the foyer into the living room to get enough space to try to revive her. They put oxygen and tubes down her throat to try to get her to breathe. They were checking her pulse, but Keenya was already dead. I had kneeled and held Keenya's hand. There was no life. The impact of the shot severed her spleen—rather I should say the bullet went into the lower part of her face, severed her spleen, and caused her to bleed to death. They covered her up with a white sheet. I stood there, staring in disbelief. This just could not be happening.

Keenya was gone.

Keenya Cook was my 21-year-old niece. She was beautiful. She was a young mother with a six-month-old baby girl. She was a daughter, a granddaughter, a niece, a cousin, and a sister. On February 16, 2002, my 14-year-old daughter opened the front door of my home near the Puyallup Indian Reservation at 2054 E 34th Street, Tacoma, Washington, and found Keenya lying on the floor. Shot brutally in the face, with a .45 caliber semi-automatic handgun; a mother, daughter, niece, cousin, and friend was murdered, killed, whatever it is we wish to call it, Keenya was gone. The sanctity of our home was now literally smoked by a dinner that would never materialize, by the burn of evil, by the smoke of the gun.

ISA FARRINGTON-NICHOLS

The First Murder Scene –REVELATION OF TRAUMA

When the police arrived they made me leave my house. They would not allow me to go back into the house because they immediately were looking to see if there was any evidence to figure out what had happened. The police and the fire department both called their chaplains in to try to console me. It was a Saturday night, and most of the detectives and coroners were off duty. They were being called at their homes regarding this crime. That was the explanation to me for having to wait. I couldn't go in the house to get clothes, I couldn't get shoes, I couldn't get my coat, I couldn't get my purse or get the baby's things. I couldn't get anything because the house, my sanctuary and Keenya's second chance, was officially a crime scene.

They began to yellow tape my door entry and a police officer stood guarding the door waiting for other law enforcement professionals to arrive. I just walked back and forth on the sidewalk in front of my front door. The door was still open. I just looked, and I stared. People in the neighborhood began to gather outside their homes, and cars began to slow down. The police began to redirect traffic and block off the intersection near my house. I just paced, waiting for detectives and coroner to arrive. They could not remove Keenya's body from the house until the coroner arrived. A few hours the coroner finally show up on the scene. They removed Keenya from the house and put her lifeless body in the ambulance where she remained until the rest of the investigators got there.

My neighbor, Mr. Aho, was the father of Tamara's best friend, Tanya. Tamara showed up at his home as I had asked her. He told me that Tamara and the baby were at his house with his daughter and wife and that they were ok. As he came to the house, I had to tell the police that he was my neighbor and that I needed his help. Mr. Aho pulled his van in front of my house and allowed me to sit in it, out of the cold, until law enforcement officers began to arrive. Hours went by before I could go anywhere. I was alone, and it was still not registering that my niece was shot and killed.

I just sat in shock. I sat distant from the world I had known. As I watched from Mr. Aho's van more and more law enforcement personnel arrived. I had watched all kinds of detective shows, and this was the central tragedy. Familiar faces began to arrive. Pamela and David, our friends, had come. They had just received word from my mother-in-law that Keenya had been hurt. They came as quickly as they could, and the police allowed them to come and talk to me. I told them that Keenya had been shot. What else could I explain? That I stopped to get information about a softball tournament? That I needed taco shells? Keenya was dead. David and Pamela cried in disbelief. I just stared at them. It was as if I could see them crying, but I could not hear them. There was nothing I could say to them. I didn't have any answers. I didn't know how, what, why, or anything.

I was approached by the fire chaplain and was told that they wanted me to sit in the detective's car. I told them that I could not go anywhere without my daughter who was at a neighbor's house. Mr. Aho went and got Tamara and the baby. When Tamara and the baby arrived, they got into the detective's car with me. The Aho's had gone to the store and bought some formula and some diapers for the baby. Tamara held the baby, who was asleep in her arms. I put my arms around them both.

We were so pitiful. We waited in the detective's car for almost another hour.

Finally, they took us down to the police station. We went down to the police station and went up to their conference room area to wait for further questioning. The police were trying to make us comfortable, offering us coffee or water. We sat there, Tamara and I, staring at each other. The baby had awakened and was looking around to make sure that we were still there. Even babies can be traumatized. Tamara told me she contacted her grandmother and told her that Keenya had been shot. She began to cry, and I was just numb. I kept trying to console my daughter, but no words would come. There were four of us girls: Keenya, Angeleah, myself, and Tamara. Four of us there under a threat that we knew nothing about. As a mother, I had been denied that role of security, nutriment, peace, love. I could not hear anything as I sat there.

The investigator and detective came and began to question Tamara and me on what happened. We explained to him how we had left her, how we arrived, and how we had found her. He asked us if we knew who could have done this. We both had no clue. They asked us about family members and their whereabouts. We told the detectives that my husband was in California and that we had not made contact with him. I had not spoken with Joseph since about 9:00 am. We also told him of Keenya's boyfriend, the baby's father, where he lived and gave the detective his name. We gave them Keenya's mother's name and information. We just answered all of their questions regarding individuals and whoever may have known Keenya, or who Keenya may have talked to or contacted that day. When we mentioned Keenya's boyfriend's name, the detective went to another room, and when he returned he showed us a picture. He asked us was that her boyfriend. Tamara had identified him by saying "yes." They informed us that he was listed as a gang member.

I didn't know much about Keenya's boyfriend, other than that Keenya had met him in high school when she was about 16. He was much older, around 8 years older, too old to be with a 16-year-old. Keenya moved in with him shortly after she turned 18. The police said that he was a thug and that he belonged to one of the local gangs. I knew that he had hit Keenya many times before, and he was very abusive to Keenya. I also knew she was afraid of what he would do. It was a very volatile relationship. I remember the night we moved Keenya's belongings from their apartment. We were very nervous. We were afraid of what he would do if he came home and saw us moving Keenya's belongings out of his apartment. I remember seeing empty cans of Old English 800 Malt Liquor. Cans were everywhere. I remember seeing some brass knuckles on the table also.

When the officer brought out his mug shot and rap sheet, I was surprised. I became very fearful because I couldn't imagine him doing something like that. It was just incomprehensible. This was his baby's mother! The detective left us in the room again. My cell phone rang and it was my husband, Joseph. I finally broke down and began to cry. I was quite relieved to hear his voice over the telephone. I needed him so much. I was so alone. I didn't want to let him go, hanging onto the phone and trying to converse so he wouldn't hang up. I figured someone had called him in California and told him about Keenya. I remember asking him to catch a flight to Tacoma. I didn't want him driving from California with him imagining Keenya there at his door, dead. I told him that Tamara and I were okay and that we were at the police station.

All he could say was, *"Isa, I'm on my way!"*

I didn't want to let him off the phone. I just needed to hear his voice. I wanted him there so badly. I felt that if he was there with me, somehow I was going to be alright. Tamara and I needed him.

Tamara and I just sat there, making the baby comfortable, still in shock at where we were, and why we were there. Someone knocked on the door, and suddenly my husband Joseph walked through the door. He was there with his brother. All I could do was stare at him like I had just seen a ghost. I was so confused. I had just spoken to him. I thought he was in California, yet there he was, within minutes walking through the door of the Police Station in Tacoma, Washington! I just sat there and stared, and I realized, I just didn't know him. He went over to Tamara and held his child. He held the baby. Our home was the burning house, and my husband was not there to save us or to get us out. I literally could not move. I just stared at them. It seemed just like the power switch from a utility company shut the power off from your house. I had just shut down. I became mute. This was going to get worse before it could ever get better.

The detectives came back into the room, looking to see who these men were. I told them it was my husband Joseph and his brother. The detective was looking quite puzzled himself because Tamara and I had just told them Joseph was in California. He didn't say anything, just shook their hands, and asked them if they wanted anything, water, coffee, and then he let them sit down. They had been to the house, and saw the house, and realized that we were no longer there. They were told that they could find us at the police station. I don't believe they were able to see Keenya's body. I had just spoken to Joseph as if he had been in California, and to have this happen in a midst of a lie only magnified the shock and hysteria. I don't know if she had been taken away from the house at that time or not. I don't know why this happened. I can only imagine what it was like for Joseph to come to his home and to see it taped off like a murder crime scene. I can only imagine what it was like for Joseph to wonder what could have possibly happened. What occurred at his home while he was "in California?"

Numbness – MY REVELATION OF HOW DARK LIFE BECOMES

We were finally allowed to leave the police station. Since our house was now an official murder scene, and we could no longer go in it, we went to my mother-in-law's home. Family members were all crying. Tamara still focused on the baby, taking care of Angeleah. I was still in a daze. I tried to explain to Joseph's family the best way I could, but I couldn't process anymore. Tamara had shared with them over the phone her details of what happened. That's probably why no one had questions for me. No one asked me any questions.

We realized that Keenya's mother was still at the Bill Cosby concert. How were we going to notify her of Keenya's tragedy? We were all worried about Keenya's mother getting the news over the television because this was a breaking news story. Reporters were still filming the house constantly. At some point, she was reached, and the news of this and her reaction required her to be taken to the hospital. I know she was in the hospital much of the early morning on Sunday, February 17th and then they released her.

ISA FARRINGTON-NICHOLS

I stayed at my mother-in-law's house for two days while we notified more family members and relatives. We notified Keenya's other grandmother who raised Keenya in the Maryland-Washington, D.C. area before Keenya came to Washington State. I contacted my family members in San Diego, California. There were so many phone calls to make, but the ultimate call was to one of my professional associates in the Pacific Northwest Chapter National Black Chamber of Commerce, Zane Fitch, who owned a mortuary. I contacted the mortuary to be prepared to get Keenya's body released from the coroner. Zane Fitch returned my call within minutes. He knew what to do.

It took days before we were allowed to go back into the house. Joseph and I eventually went back to our house. There was blood. Her violent departure from this earth was marked at the mouth of our home. It is what awaited me as I entered. I began to remember in my mind the images of finding Keenya the night of the murder. Keenya's bloodstains in the foyer entry and on the living room carpet stamped her last resting spot. The bloodstains showed where they had pulled her when they were trying to revive her. There were splashes of her blood on the walls. The house still had the awful stench of smoke. The house was pretty much ruined with the smoke smell from the burning stove. When I looked into the pot, the chicken that Keenya was boiling had just disintegrated, and the pot had melted and was just stuck. There was yellow tape around the doorway and Xs and markings on the floor. Several detectives were still talking to neighbors, canvassing the property, the grounds, and the alleys looking for clues, looking for information that would not only bring justice but maybe peace of mind.

RESTORE

The home had become devoid of the sanctity or unity to truly heal from this tragedy. This was our first home and we had to live in it after this tragedy. Joseph and I tried to put our relationship together, we also tried to put our home back together again. This is where we sent our daughter away to attend St. Augustine's University. This is also where we brought her twin baby girls home from Madigan Army Medical Hospital. A new generation had entered this home after such a tragedy. We watched our daughter, Tasheera, become a mother from this very home. We had to get our lives together. Home is where the heart is. Yet with time, I realized Joseph's heart was no longer in the home. It made him easier to be away from me, in his version of California.

Messages were left by family, friends, and reporters. We listened to each one, and I remembered all the bloodstains as each voicemail closed with a beep. One day in this sea of an emotional abyss, there was a knock on the door. More detectives had come by the house. I opened the door, and I let them in. They were quite professional, and as I hung up the phone they were waiting to ask us some more questions. They informed us that they had not been successful in finding Keenya's boyfriend. They had been out to his house and asked if we knew of any other place we could find him. My husband and I didn't know anything else to tell them. Just as their questions were asked, the telephone rang with their answer. It was DeAngelo, the baby's father.

"Hello is Keenya there?"

I looked at Joseph, who answered the call, and Joseph said that DeAngelo was asking to speak to Keenya. I took the phone to speak with DeAngelo.

"DeAngelo, we have been looking for you. Everyone has been looking for you. Keenya has been shot."

I didn't tell him Keenya was dead. DeAngelo said that he was on his way to our home. The detectives immediately notified the police to move their cars, and I began to look at my husband with nervousness. We just didn't know what to expect. The detectives said that they would just wait, but they radioed for everyone to clear the street, so as not to draw attention that something was wrong or cause DeAngelo not to come to our house. The detectives and officers, who were positioned nearby, prepared for DeAngelo's arrival.

DeAngelo arrived with his friend as Joseph answered the door. They came into the house, into the bloodied entryway. DeAngelo immediately noticed the violent splatters on the floor and grabbed his head with both of his hands in anguish. As he came towards the kitchen, the detectives stepped up.

"What happened?" cried DeAngelo.

The detectives informed him that they wanted to speak with him. DeAngelo arrived and without understanding what had even happened, detectives put DeAngelo in handcuffs and took him down to the station.

Joseph reassured DeAngelo that we all had been questioned, that we all had been down to the police station. I was so nervous because I just didn't know DeAngelo and the fact that someone would murder Keenya left me just wondering if we were still in danger.

We were not aware of why they decided to handcuff DeAngelo then. They could have questioned him without handcuffs just as we had been questioned. The fact that the detectives showed us DeAngelo's mug shot and said that he was a member of the

RESTORE

neighborhood Crips gang, just left a very horrid feeling in my stomach at the possibility of Keenya's murder being gang-related. What could Keenya possibly have done to anyone that they would want to kill her?

While we were still at the house, I began to wonder and ask myself: "How in the heck am I going to clean up this house? Keenya's blood was everywhere."

I asked the female detective, *"How do you clean up stuff like this?"*

She went to the patrol car and gave me a business card of a company named *Bio-Clean*. She told me they were very good and police departments used them to clean murder scenes frequently. I took the business card and stuck it in my pocket. I was quite relieved that there was a resource that I could call to start the process of getting my home cleaned up.

I just put the card in my pocket for a later day, whenever I would be ready to deal with cleaning. Someday I would have to deal with getting the house cleaned up. I would have to restore it to be home, and that would require every member of the home to participate. But not at that moment. We headed back to my mother-in-law's house. I checked in with my baby girl, Tamara. Tamara was still taking care of baby Angeleah. She would not leave her alone. She was quiet most of the time, but I felt that her taking care of the baby was consoling her in some way. I felt that they were consoling each other. Most of the family members were now at my mother-in-law's house, and it was becoming very crowded because it was only a 2-bedroom apartment. Some eight people were all there in that 2-bedroom apartment.

Joseph shared with everyone how DeAngelo had been taken away for questioning, but Keenya's mom couldn't imagine him killing her child. The pain and the shock of this entire ordeal were just beginning to settle in on us. Despair and grief were imminent in everyone. The suddenness of Keenya's departure without motive, nor a known enemy or reason, gave her departure a mysterious gloom. Keenya's mother was just reeking with pain, in tears and fears for what had happened to her child, her baby. Keenya was her youngest child, her baby girl, and then having to look at little Angeleah, her 6-month-old granddaughter, made it more horrific.

We witnessed a six-month-old baby grieve. You could see on her face as she was so diligently looking for her mother to appear. At the mention of her mother's name, she would look around. Every time someone said Keenya around the baby, she would stop whatever she was doing, and look to see if it was her mommy. Sometimes I wondered if Keenya's spirit was around. Sometimes it felt like there was her presence in the room. I never said anything about feeling this energy in the room, but I paid close attention to the baby's constant motion of looking into open space as if someone was standing beside her, and she would start crying. That was unbelievable to me. Other people began to notice that the baby would look around and stare at a location or space in the room and start crying. I remember getting the baby and holding her, and she stared at me, and I looked into her little eyes, and she put her arm around my neck. I just held her like I used to do every day that she was with me in my very home. As I walked around the room, she just laid her head on my shoulder. I began to pat her softly on her shoulder, and she began to pat me on mine.

RESTORE

The Fourth Day After the Murder — REVELATION OF IDENTITY

It was now February 20th, the fourth day after the murder. I got a call from the police. They wanted to talk to Joseph, Tamara, and me for more questioning down at the police station. We went back down there. They took Tamara to a room, and we waited outside. I noticed that we now had new detectives in charge of the case. They introduced themselves and told us that they would be working on Keenya's case from that point on. It was two white male cops, a Detective Webb and another whose name I forget. Eventually, it was my turn to go in, and the detectives began to interrogate. They asked me questions and asked me to repeat what had happened. They were particularly interested in my husband's whereabouts on the night of Keenya's murder. I told them that I thought he was in California, and I found out that night that he had not gone to California. Of course, they had a field day with this.

The interrogation room was like the set of *Law and Order*. There was a long conference table where I was sitting in one chair, and two white male police officers sat across the table from me. One would ask questions, while the other would observe my expressions. Then the other would ask questions, while the other would analyze. They took turns. I kept feeling like they were trying to make up a story, rather than allowing me to tell the story. Their line of questioning was very personal, but I had nothing to hide. All I knew was that Joseph and his brother had left for a short vacation for the weekend. All I know is that he called me that morning and said that he had arrived safely in California and would call me back when he got settled. The detectives felt that something was terribly wrong and that there may be a reason that someone was there to kill me instead of Keenya.

"*Do you know why your husband would lie?*"

"*Why would he tell you he was in one place when he was in another?*"

I honestly had no explanation and was forced to reexamine my marriage in an interrogation room. I told them they should ask him that question, that he would be better suited to answer it because I just didn't know. Joseph is a liar, but that doesn't make him a killer.

"*Were you aware that an insurance policy had been taken out on you just before the murder?*"

I told them I was aware of one policy and it was a policy that we had for 20 years. It was a term insurance policy that we had gotten right after we had our first child and that policy was still in force. I looked at them, and I asked them with whom was the policy? They told me that they could not release that information because of the on-going investigation.

The detectives began to play good cop, bad cop. The good cop would be very consoling and understanding, and then the bad cop would be hard and make it plain that they were going to find out exactly who killed Keenya, and that they did not give a care about any of us. He didn't use the word care. Instead, he used a filthy word that was not warranted. It was unprofessional and inconsiderate. After the bad cop said that, I took offense by his demeanor and statement. I pay property taxes which helped pay his salary. His job was to find Keenya's killer. If it means he needed to start with the investigation of my personal life, then he needed to just get it over with. Once again, I reiterated I had nothing to hide. They continued to question me about whether or not my husband was having an affair.

I admitted, *"Yes, he has had affairs before!"*

They wanted to know if I felt that he was having an affair the night Keenya was killed. I told them I wasn't sure, that he could have, and that I did not know his whereabouts. I reiterated that this exact question was something only Joseph could answer. The detectives continued playing nice cop/bad cop. The nice cop reassured me of his role and responsibility to seeking justice, truth, and peace of mind. They claimed to see this type of stuff every day, and they had to be this way. Regardless of their harshness and the tone of their voice, they were there to do their job in finding Keenya's killer. Once again, I agreed that I too wanted them to do their job!

They then asked me one of the most appalling questions.

"Do you think your husband was sleeping with Keenya?"

I had had enough! Of course, they looked at my every expression and my reaction.

"No, I don't feel that my husband was sleeping with Keenya!"

"How could you be sure; how could you say that?"

In my mind, I had no way of being absolutely sure, but I didn't want to think of the fact that Joseph could have been sleeping with Keenya. I don't feel that my husband would do anything like that, anything of that nature with his very own niece. I was going to vomit. What was a lie between a husband and a wife grew into a lie that police detectives questioned for a murder investigation. The detectives continued to dwell on the fact of my apparent failing marriage, and they began to pressure me into thinking that this could be the cause of Keenya's death. The murderer was coming after me and that this was a case of mistaken identity.

ISA FARRINGTON-NICHOLS

I did not understand why Joseph would lie. I didn't understand what reason he would have for being in one place and telling me something else. Often in our relationship, when he went out he would just not come home. When he came home, he would make up some story that he was with his brother or hanging out with the 'fellas'. We would surely argue. I never liked it or appreciated it when he would leave and not come home. He would not call to say he was okay or that he wasn't coming home. I would be up all night worried, angry, and sometimes crying.

They asked me why I would stay. How could I stay married to a liar and a cheater? The interrogator even said that his wife would not tolerate that type of behavior. I told him that's why she is his wife, and I am Joseph's wife. I said I have a gift to forgive. I forgave, and we went on with our lives. They asked me how many affairs he had of which I was aware. I told them several. I was not naïve and there were probably some that I didn't know. Being a soldier in the military on deployment from your family would make it impossible for me to know what he would be doing.

Detective Webb asked how many affairs have I had. Joseph and I had separated in 1992. I saw another person casually during the separation. I dated for companionship, but it would not last. I was emotionally connected to Joseph. I could never get over the love I had for my husband. He was the love of my life. We both had seen other people during our separation. In 1999, we reconciled and I had no other relationships after our reconciliation. The names Cecil Stewman, Stanley Barnes, and Tony Wright came up. The police had asked if they were lovers of mine.

"So what do they represent in your life?"

RESTORE

Cecil is a good friend of my father, myself, and my entire family. I explained that we were close and he would help me with my disabled father. As a friend, I cared about him. I explained that these people were friends and business associates of mine. Tony Wright was my business partner of seven years. We were Nichols, Wright, and Associates. It was apparent to me that the detectives had been questioning other family members and these names were given to them.

The detectives returned the questioning to my faltering marriage again. I couldn't help but think that there was possibly some woman who would want to kill me so that she could have full access to my husband. Joseph had returned to his patterns of being gone all night. The detectives told me that the things that we see on television are the things they see in their line of work every day. All of the questions that they asked me about the insurance policy being taken out on me, my husband's infidelities, and our finances, were all perfectly sound motives for murder.

When I left the station, I realized that the constant questioning had gone on for three and a half hours. I walked out, and my character was defamed. Areas in my marriage that I had ignored or tried to overlook were now at the center of my thoughts. Areas that although were shattered and fragile, now were obviously and forever broken. Joseph was in the lobby full of sorrow, and we all went back over to his mother's house.

Tamara went back into the house while Joseph and I just sat there outside in the car. I was so confused. I tried to look at his eyes and looked for anything that connected him to this tragedy in any kind of way. Perhaps there, in the space of his eyes, there was a danger I had not noticed before. Could this be a fatal attraction from one of his affairs? As I peered into the eyes of the man I had married, the man I called my husband, the father of my daughters, all I could see was a hurt and damaged liar. I could see guilt, pain, and anger. I wonder what he saw when he looked back into my eyes. I felt fear, betrayal, and anger. I felt alone and abandoned. I felt worthless. I wondered if he could see any of those things when he looked into my eyes. Did he even care for how I felt? Even through all of that, I somehow still felt love for him. Joseph and I had very few words to say. The communication that was much needed was gone. So, I remained silent. He did the same.

Keenya's Funeral — MY REVELATION OF ACTS OF KINDNESS

We returned to my house that afternoon to make funeral arrangements. Keenya's body was finally going to be released to the funeral home. I had contacted *Destiny Center Ministries*, the church that I attended, and I contacted *St. John Baptist Church*, the church for which my father was a deacon.

When I first called Mr. Fitch, he wasn't there, however called me back a short time later. He handled all the arrangements with the coroner in getting the body released. He was also aware that we didn't have any money to bury Keenya. I told him that I had resources that I was looking into that would pay for Keenya's services. He said he was familiar with the one I had chosen. It was called *Victims of Violent Crime*. There's a process you go through, and Keenya qualified to receive the victim's compensation funding that would pay for the funeral. Mr. Fitch had worked with this organization before, and he was able to get the paperwork started once I gave him a case number. He explained to me how they worked and that they would pay him for his services.

Mr. Fitch was just awesome. I notified the family, and we began to work with him on Keenya's funeral. *Victims of Violent Crime* is a nonprofit organization that provides a variety of services, including counseling, financial support, burial assistance, and advocacy to any victim, whether he or she is a survivor or a fatality. I had contacted the local chapter for the Pierce County, Washington area, and was asked for the police case number. I was given a claim number. Once I got the claim number, I gave it to Mr. Fitch, who was now able to handle the funeral arrangements. What Mr. Fitch did for our family was incredible. Because he was in charge of the funeral directing, he could wait for his payment, but the cemetery had to be paid in advance of Keenya's burial. Mr. Fitch wrote the cemetery a check for me. For this, I am so grateful. Although we were still obligated to reimburse the mortuary for payment, we were compiling our resources to get the funds together. Friends and the people that heard of the tragedy began to give money to help cover expenses.

Zane [Fitch], who had specialized in serving victims of violence, was very much appreciated by me. He stepped up and was involved, sought out information, and took on a role I never expected. I realized that he had done pro bono work regularly and put in a lot of extra work that he had not billed us for. He even went so far as to include an extra limousine so that the entire family could have transportation for the funeral. He was quite consoling yet very professional in addressing the trauma and the toll of the tragedy on me personally. I appreciated the work and the support that he provided to me and to the family in the time of our immediate bereavement and need.

The funeral arrangements kept me busy. I was not able to touch the surface of the multiple shocks that hit my household with this tragedy. I wanted the funeral to represent how sorry and sad I felt about losing Keenya in my home. I wanted my pain and sadness to be a celebration of love because Keenya was loved and will be forever loved. I wanted the funeral to be a memorial of how beautiful and how special she was to me and our family. I wanted to disassociate Keenya's funeral from the horror of what happened to her, the tragedy of her death, and somehow try to find the peace and grace that she was now with the Savior, that she was resting, finally. Making the funeral arrangement was the solstice for me. I gave a lot of updates back to the family on the funeral arrangements, being very careful to get what they wanted for the arrangements. One of the things I decided to do was to design and write Keenya's obituary. It would be something Angeleah would have to remember her mother by and read when she was old enough. It to be a keepsake to send to everyone who loved Keenya to see what a gift she was and that we had been blessed with the perfect gift, baby Angeleah.

I started the obituary with the sunrise of Keenya being born, the first day she was taken home and put into her older sister's arms to hold. There was a snapshot that I had found of baby Keenya, a few days old, in the arms of her six-year-old sister. I used that picture to introduce Keenya on one cover of the obituary. In the center of the obituary, I used a picture of Angeleah by herself. Underneath the picture of Angeleah was a poem, a poem that was in a sense from Keenya to Angeleah. I

RESTORE

used to be the Mistress of Ceremony Poetry Slams, which are poetry competitions. I started to write one evening when the baby was on my heart. The emotions of my trauma built tears that clouded my eyes. I could not finish the poem, so I called a friend of mine who was a poet. I read to my poet friend what I wrote, and I sent it to him so he could read what I wrote. I told him how I had to say this because I didn't have a way to let the baby know about her mom. I wanted to finish it, but the tears drowned my vision and words in a way that was so painful. He, along with another poet and friend, finished the poem.

ISA FARRINGTON-NICHOLS

"The Mother's Song of Angeleah"

Baby, cry if you must…
But don't cry long.
My song is sung beside you
In a forever chorus –
A force to guide you
Through these loving days,
To comfort and protect you
As you grow and play.
In my autumn way
I am lifting you gently
I am the wind in your spring
I will sing you back
Into summer's warmth
And lay with you into the safe
Hearth of returning winters.
For no one knows the hour
No one knows the time
When they will be called

RESTORE

To be with the Most High …
The divine
We find strength in things not seen
We hope of things to come…knowing
That there's a place waiting for us
In the everlasting kingdom.
Settle into rest,
My tender Angeleah;
Nestle into love,
My gentle Angeleah.
When the branch flickers
In the steady wind,
It is me,
When the rain dances
Down your path,
When the sun soaks
Your soulful hair,
Your mother is in the air.
So fear not my precious
Angeleah, (for) I have gone nowhere,
For as long as you live…So too do I.
My song – it lives inside you…
A mother's lullaby.

ISA FARRINGTON-NICHOLS

The third picture was a photo of Keenya smiling, her hair down her back. Underneath Keenya's photo was the story of her life with her new baby. The passing of Keenya was related to a symbolic sunset, and I used a picture that resembled how she appeared most of the time. She was beautiful and charismatic. On the back, I was thinking about what I could say about Keenya, and I began with scripture from the *Book of James*, 1:17

> "Every good and perfect gift is from above, coming down from the Father of the heavenly lights...."

As I began to reminiscence that Keenya was a gift to every individual who shared in her life, this verse came to mind. I wanted others to realize that Keenya was leaving us a special gift, a gift of joy and love, and that gift was her six-month-old daughter, Angeleah Ashani Yves Rogers.

Keenya was truly a gift to everyone and me as well. The fourth and final picture was one we had just taken four months ago around Thanksgiving with the entire family, the last picture that we had taken as a family before Keenya's murder. I used that picture on the final page of the obituary. I did the acknowledgment of condolences, special thanks to different people, and thanks to people that helped us during our time of grief. I remember thanking friends like Candace, Jean, and Addie. I remember thanking the management staff of *Fashion Bug*, the store where Keenya worked. I remember thanking the poets, Lucas Smiraldo and his friend, Paul. I remember thanking Robin Henderson, my friend at *Key Bank* for setting up a "Contribution Trust Fund Account" for Keenya's baby. I remember thanking *Destiny Center Ministries*. I remember thanking *St. John Baptist Church*, John Leach, and Laser Writing.

RESTORE

John Leach was the man that put the obituary together. He was the typesetter and printer. You could tell he put his compassion for my family's loss, into his work. I remember thanking Zane Fitch and the *Upper Room Mortuary* and *Mountain View Cemetery*. I remember thanking Carrie from *Victims of Violent Crime*. I remember thanking the Tacoma Police Department and the Tacoma Fire Department for their assistance the day Keenya was murdered.

After I thanked all these individuals in writing on behalf of the family of Keenya Cook, it was my prayer that the Lord would bless every one of them. I prayed that He would keep them, shine His face on each one of them and be gracious to them, and give them all peace.

The obituary was to be my atonement for the tragedy that took place at our home. It was interesting because, before the final print of the obituary, I had made sure that I had all the input from the Nichols' family. We had the obituary being read by me. We had the musical selections by Keenya's aunt and her very best friend from high school. We had the acknowledgments and remarks by another aunt. We had both pastors – one from my church and from my church that I attended for six years. I provided a draft of the obituary to the family to look at and to read.

They commented on how beautiful it was and that they appreciated my efforts. I looked at their faces of grief. Another prayer came to my mind. I remember getting into someplace quiet and writing the prayer down. As a final remark, I stood up at the funeral and I read this prayer. It was a prayer request for the family called, "The Power of Prayer".

ISA FARRINGTON-NICHOLS

The power of prayer, that prayer from the righteous availeth much. Prayer can change things, and prayer can enter into places no one else can go. I said that when you pray for a family, I ask for people to pray on these things: that no weapon formed against us would prosper; that GOD would set free, heal, and deliver each of us; that the Lord is the strength of our life; that the GOD of our Lord Jesus Christ, the Father of Glory, gives to each of us the spirit of wisdom, and revelation in the knowledge of HIM; that GOD would continue to bless each of us and to keep us. I asked that people pray for the husbands in our family; that they would love themselves, therefore loving their wives more than themselves. I asked people to pray that the men in our family would stand and be the men of GOD according to their purpose. I asked people to pray for the wives of our family, that we would be the helpmeet that GOD ordained for our husbands. I asked people to pray that we would be submissive unto our husbands. I asked that people pray that the covenant that GOD joined for our marriages, that no man or woman could put asunder. I asked the people at the funeral to pray for the single women in our family, that GOD loving, Holy Spirit-filled men would come into their lives, and that, until such a time, that they remain in a close relationship with GOD, our Father. I asked everyone at the funeral to pray for our children, that grace and mercy would be forever with them, that they be raised to be obedient, to honor their parents, so that their days would be long on the earth. I asked the people at the funeral that they would pray that we would find peace that our family would find love, and joy, that our family will rejoice in the Lord always.

So many people wanted to know what they could do for me. All I could come up with was prayer. I needed prayer. I was raised in a house of prayer. My daddy and mama always prayed no matter what happened. So prayer was what we did in good times and impossible times. The entire family needed prayer! Joseph and I were in turmoil. We were in a lot of pain and sorrow. It was a time we could have never imagined we would be in. The shock was traumatic and there was nothing we could do to console each other. It was his wife and youngest child there that dreadful day. Keenya's mother was our focus. I tried hard to console my sister-in-law. Her heart was broken. Her baby girl was gone forever.

As the procession for the final viewing of Keenya's body, it was the final goodbye to a beautiful young woman. Those who were in attendance slowly walked single file in procession around her casket. One by one, friends walked slowly to pay their respect to Keenya and the family. Once everyone had proceeded out of the church, the door was closed and it was time for the family to say goodbye. DeAngelo's mother, grandfather, and sister were in attendance. They were in remorse. They genuinely loved Keenya and the baby. DeAngelo's mother repeatedly cried out that her son did not do this, her son did not do this! I can imagine the pain at the fact that this had happened, and that her son at the time was the police's #1 suspect. DeAngelo was detained at the station for a parole violation, and he was not in attendance for the funeral.

It was now the end of the public viewing recession and time for the family viewing. It was quite difficult because she lay there looking so innocent. When I walked up to the casket I looked down at her for the final time. I had seen her when she lay on the floor in my home. I had seen her when she arrived at the mortuary from the coroner. I was there when her body was being dressed for her services. I took a deep breath and released it.

I looked down at her beautiful face, I closed my eyes. I knew I was falling. I could feel the impact of all of this culminating in my body. I tried to get my knees to support me. I could tell I needed to decompress, but the hemorrhaging from within after so much trauma had grown. When I saw her face, I fell. I dropped to the floor.

Keenya was there like a princess. No one could tell how violently she had passed. The marking of the bullet was gone.

The Nichols family were consoling one another as much as we could. It was time to go to the cemetery to complete the burial. It was the usual Northwest rain outside. We rode in the limousines through the neighborhood along with a processional of cars. I was so exhausted, I sat in the car during the burial. I was feeling euphoric and dizzy. I watched my niece being laid in her final resting spot from the limousine window. I watched in support of my children.

Keenya's uncles were carrying her casket, and from the car window, I watched the progression of her burial. As they set her to her final place, his shoe got stuck in the mud. His size 15 shoes were sucked into the mud of rainy Washington. They didn't know if he was fainting or if that was the reason why he was staggering. Days and days of rain and mud had given relief as I watched their silent chuckles from behind the car window glass, watching him get his shoe back on, to continue the burial.

We returned to the church for the repast with family and friends. During the repast, there were many people there to console the family. Some people presented sympathy cards with cash. I wanted people to remember that we had set up "Angeleah's Contributions Trust Fund Account" at *Key Bank* for

RESTORE

donations. This baby would grow up without her mother and not knowing the fate of her father.

Friends and Community – MY REVELATION THAT MONEY IS NOT GOING TO CHANGE ANYTHING

I felt that "Angeleah's Contributions Trust Fund Account" in the baby's name, with her uncle Joseph, my husband, as the executor, would help possibly provide money to send the baby to college someday. One of my clients and friends, Robin Henderson, was a banking officer at *Key Bank*. She set up the account so that anyone could go in and make a contribution to that account. We had this information to give to anybody in hopes that the media would broadcast it on the airways as they were covering the story.

The media was in frenzy. They camped outside of our front door for three weeks. We were the breaking news story in the Tacoma-Seattle area for two weeks as Police continued to find and look for clues and updates on the mysterious murder of Keenya Cook. I remember praying because of all of the hurt, and all of the rumors and gossip and speculation that were going around. The media was at the funeral as well as the Tacoma Police Department detectives looking at the rawest of emotions from different people in attendance, and trying to look for clues, and look at any possible connection to Keenya's killer.

I gave an interview with media supervisors and gave explicit instruction that their use of my story would be to announce the trust information. But, unbeknownst to me, the media said very little about the trust account, and deliberately used the interview to gain listeners for their agenda. It was apparent that they were only interested in selling the sensation of the story. The story of the murder and the trauma of the tragedy were selling points rather than points for charity and kindness.

All five networks had production vehicles on all four corners of the house, waiting to talk to anyone, mainly myself. After my experience with the reporter who took my story as something to sell, I no longer trusted the media. I stayed away from them. I was the only one who felt that way. The Nichols family appeared many times in the paper. The media was consistently capturing their raw feelings of hurt, anger, and confusion. It was all over the news. There was so much speculation as to who could have committed this crime, and the media was hanging onto every thread of dialogue, every word that they could pick up on for the story. The police had assigned a Public Relations person from their department to give media updates. Yet, the investigation was just beginning. Tacoma news media covered the murder from the time it was called into 911. It was broadcasted as a breaking news story that interrupted regularly schedule programming in Tacoma almost all day, every day. The entire community recognized our home on the news showing yellow tape around the entire corner block while police officers walked around the house exterior looking for clues and evidence. It was a very scary and uncomfortable time in our lives.

Eventually, DeAngelo was released from custody. He had been rigorously interrogated and given a lie detector or polygraph, and he passed it. The detectives told me they were pretty sure that he had not committed the murder. The police then started canvassing and revisiting witnesses. As they were taking these statements, and as bits and pieces of information were getting into the press, the press would contact members of the family, and whoever would open their mouth to talk to them they would publish in the paper or broadcast. At that time, I had no clue as to who could have done this to my niece, and for that reason, I found it most appropriate to stay away from the media.

The police investigation was not going well at all because they were focusing on Joseph and me. The investigators continued to pursue their thoughts of someone coming for me. They questioned whether my daughter was involved in any gang activities or had any enemies. They were making assumptions that this was a retaliation of some sort of mistaken identity.

Life Interrupted and Homeless - MY REVELATION OF HOW MUCH I LOST

I had left my mother-in-law's house and accepted an invitation from my dearest friend, Linda Braddy, while my home was still in a crime scene shamble. Linda was not able to attend the funeral, but she gave me access to her home. I started the process of *RESTORING* my life and home. I found the business card of the cleaning company that the detective referred to me. I contacted them, and they immediately returned my call and met me at my home. I went to the house alone that particular evening to meet with them. I circled the block to see if there were any reporters parked near. I had spent much time these past years worried about people outside, whether it was John or now these reporters. After making sure no media was around, I went into the house, and I pulled the car into the garage and waited. When they finally arrived, I was surprised to see two white women who owned this business. They were very professional and very compassionate. They came in, and I was so glad to see them. I wanted very much to clean the blood up from Keenya's wound. They had performed the cleanup for the Nicole Simpson and Ron Goldman crime scene in Brentwood, California. That right there let me know that they were the experts in the field and handled high profile crime scenes. I sat on the staircase, two steps above where Keenya's head laid as they assessed the cleanup that needed to be done. They put on overalls and gloves. They had different types of tools and supplies. I remember asking one of them if I needed to be covered up, and their reply was "only if I wanted to help them do the cleaning."

I laughed and kindly said, "Thank you but no thank you!"

I thought to myself about my first instinct to get a carpet cleaner and a mop and just mop the floors myself. Boy, was I naïve. This was actually a job for professionals. There was no way I could have cleaned the house the proper way it had to be cleaned. I sat there on the staircase and watched them clean, and I began to ask them questions about their line of work. Not only did they clean crime scenes, but they were also called quite a bit to clean all kinds of contaminations. They had an abundant amount of methamphetamine labs to clean in the Pierce County area. They told me those cleaning methamphetamine labs in any building structure have to gut the premise out completely, including the walls and the floors, to get rid of those types of chemical contaminants. They cleaned for almost three hours.

As I stood there, I watched them remove every plank up from the hardwood floors one by one. When they picked up the plank, it had been at least three weeks since Keenya's murder, and the plank from the hardwood floor was still moist and saturated with blood. The blood had penetrated deep into the foundation of my home, almost two feet to the foyer of the hallway.

RESTORE

Keenya's blood became a part of my foundation. She had bled to death. I was thinking that the blood was only going to be in the area where her head laid, where the trauma was most apparent. Yet the blood had traveled so far, and 26 planks of wood were lifted to reveal her blood still soaking there. They took all those wood planks up until you could see the concrete slab of the floor, upon which they sprayed a solution. Then they took the carpet area and just cut around the bloodied area of the carpet, basically in the shape of where Keenya's body laid.

The blood came to be in the carpet when the paramedics moved her from the original location, into the living room where they tried to revive her. They cut that carpet until you could see the concrete on the floor and then they sprayed it with more of this special decontaminating solution. They explained to me that blood is so contaminating that Keenya could have had an infectious disease and not been aware that she was infected, and that the contamination of blood would still be in carpet fibers, wood planks, and walls. The solution they were using was a solution that kills bacteria and prevents the spread of contamination. They then began to spray the walls and ceiling. They saw blood splatters that I had never even noticed. Keenya's blood was a mosaic painting over our hopes and desires.

There was a knock at the door. It was my friend, Leroy, who decided to stop by when he saw lights on in the house. I opened the door, and we sat on the stairway and conversed as they continued to clean. He mentioned that I was in his prayers, and he wanted to see if there was anything I needed. I said that I could use a shot of Brandy. He said he'd be right back. He came back and knocked on the door with a small pint of Brandy. We poured a glass, and we sat on the stairway while the cleaning team continued to work. We marveled at how this could have happened to Keenya.

The cleaning team finished yet there still was much work to be done. The next day I was contacted by *State Farm Insurance Company*. Reggie Johnson, our insurance agent, came and gave condolences because they had seen the house on the news and immediately my insurance agent recognized that we were his clients. When he arrived he was compassionate and wanted to do whatever he could to ensure aspects of our home insurance were clear and simple. The insurance company gave us a list of contractors that were licensed. I gave that information to Joseph so that he could contact them. All we had to do was pay the deductible and they started right away.

After it was all said and done, they replaced the kitchen appliances, re-layered the hardwood floors, and put in new carpet. They also had the vents cleaned for smoke, and paid to have the furniture professionally cleaned to see if the bloodstains would come out, but they were unsuccessful. Those bloodstains would not come out. Even with all the scrubbing, the memories would remain. They ended up giving us money to replace our furniture. They paid to dry clean all of the clothing in the house since the stench of smoke was in all of our clothing. Joseph and I used the money to try to rebuild our home. I found out later that his family wanted to know where we were getting money from. They thought we took a policy out on Keenya. Can you believe that? That is what media does to families.

We were able to order a garage door opener and a new screen door with locks. We wondered that if we had such things that perhaps this could have all been avoided. Somehow perhaps Keenya could have been spared. If there was a storm door between her and the person on the porch, Angeleah may have never been left crying upstairs, unattended. I remember driving around my neighborhood and Linda's neighborhood. I noticed that many of the front doors lacked screen doors. Some doors had storm doors, but most doors had nothing. I would start thinking about ways that could have possibly saved Keenya's life. We put in a light sensor and a video camera to see who was approaching our front door. We wanted to increase our security when we moved back into our home. I realized that our sense of security would never, ever be the same. Our ability to feel secure would never be *RESTORED*. It took almost 45 days before the contractor completed the renovation on the damages. We did not know who killed Keenya or why Angeleah was destined to lose her mother at such a young age, but at least the smoke was gone.

A Friend Indeed to a Friend in Need – MY REVELATION THAT YOU CAN RELY TOO MUCH ON YOUR FRIENDS

I took solitude at Linda's home. Linda lived on the north end of Tacoma in a comfortable, split-level home with all the amenities of a warm abode. There was exercise equipment. There was healthy food. There were vitamins. There was a television, stereos, and a fireplace. It was the perfect place to be still and to begin the process of healing. Linda holds a special place in my heart. She was heading to Las Vegas for that softball tournament that we played in every year. I had airline tickets to go as well. Before Linda left, she went to the funeral home with me when Keenya's body was released. Linda's being there while I was the only other one there to view Keenya's body was, in my mind, indicative of God's timing. Linda and I viewed Keenya's body together, and we held hands, and we prayed. Shortly thereafter the mortuary staff began to prep Keenya for the funeral. Linda then left to catch her flight, a flight I should have been on, playing softball with my team. I had no idea I had people in my life that were so caring and awesome. God put wings on Linda that day. I had no one there for me. Not anyone.

Linda's routine of healthy eating and exercise was mandatory. Little did I know that it was saving my life! Saving me from an actual emotional and psychological breakdown. She had me focus on staying healthy because the exercise was going to help with my major depression. My main function was to get up, get dressed, and get out. If I could only get up, get dressed and get out, I could make it to the next day. Another convenience of being at Linda's house was that it was just a few blocks from the middle school that Tamara was bussed to from our East Side Tacoma home.

Tamara attended this particular school and was bussed there because it was a school for highly capable learners. Tamara was one. Linda had extended her home to my entire family, but Joseph had chosen to stay somewhere else, which was something I was used to anyways. Occasionally, he would come and spend the night. Linda was so wonderful that I could talk when I needed to talk. I could cry when I felt like crying, but she was careful not to let me wallow for too long. She always redirected my energy into taking care of me. By taking care of me, Tamara was under my umbrella.

By March 16th, it was 30 days into the investigation, and Joseph and I were still not communicating regularly. The infidelity issue was like an elephant in a small room; a subject matter that we tiptoed around for years. One early evening he had taken me to Linda's house. We sat in the car, and we discussed the night of the murder. He explained to me that he was with his friend Will, and he didn't know why he led me to believe that they were gone. He told me that they had meant to leave, and decided at some point, not to go.

"Why did you call me that morning and allow me to think that you were out of town? How you could say that you arrived in California? Why couldn't you have just said that you were just leaving, or you were still on the road, or you had decided not to go? What's the big deal?"

Our voices began to get loud. The anger had finally oozed out and broke through like a boil filled with pus. It was a festering boil that had infected the entire marriage and our home. I began to tell him how horrible I felt being interrogated by a white police officer who told me my husband was a liar and asked me what kind of wife, what kind of woman, would stay married to a man who would lie and cheat on her. I screamed at him and told him how degrading and dirty I felt as those white police officers kept asking me if I was having affairs with someone.

"You, Joseph, said that I had been having an affair?!"

I was angry that Joseph would leave our home unprotected while he chose to be out partying with his friends. Why would partying with his friends be more important than being at home with Tamara and me? Was our life, our marriage, so horrible for him that he had to plan stories of being out of town just to get away from me, to get away from home?

His answers didn't make sense to me. It just wasn't enough. It wasn't until a few months later I found out this information by way of his youngest sister. Joseph was with a woman named Brenda. Everyone in his family knew that he was still in town except for me. And they knew why. I was devastated and disgusted.

In October 1999 we reconciled from a three-year separation. Joseph returned from his third Korean tour of duty and came back to me. By 2001, he had returned to the streets, returned to his usual episodes of disappearing, staying out, and excluding me. It's now February 2002, and I can't help but wonder why I was back here. What was my lesson to learn? It was so unusual for him to go to such extremes because he had partied with his friends before, all night long, not returning home till the next morning sometimes. What was so different this time that he would have to tell me that he was in another town, in another state.

The pain was much more than we both could imagine. He too had been interrogated and called a liar, a cheat. The police accused him of sleeping with his niece. He had to also share this information with the military personnel. His 17-year military service in the United States Army was on the line.

I had no answers. I didn't feel any better. I still felt that something was missing. It was just too extreme. I got out of the car and went into the house, took a shower, and cried myself to sleep. The investigation was still going on. My house was just about finished with the repairs and the renovations from the murder, and it was time to return home. I left most of the renovation oversight to Joseph. I left all the communicating with the press to Joseph. He was the spokesperson for the Joseph Nichols family. I just had no words to say. God just literally closed my vocal cords. I was almost spiritually and emotionally comatose.

RESTORE

A Wilderness Wandering – MY REVELATION OF MENTAL HEALTH

By March 26th, it had been a little over 40 days and the house was almost finished with the restoration. It was time to go back to our home. The neighbors from the community had left flowers and cards of condolences. People had lit candles and placed them on our porch. There were bouquets and plants everywhere. I remember turning on the TV at Linda's house and seeing news clips of our home and a neighbor walking up the pathway with a gift and placing it on the porch and then leaving. The neighborhood was fairly quiet most of the time. I lived right on the bus line and our neighborhood was ethnically diverse. We lived within Puyallup Native American Reservation in the City of Tacoma, Washington. The neighbors' response to the tragedy was very consoling. They too had been praying for our household. A neighbor named Heidi, who I had never met before, left a book of prayers. Inside the book, she wrote the warmest expression of condolence to my family. I wanted to meet her, but I never did.

Most of the neighbors had been interviewed by the detectives. The detectives were in the area daily looking for clues and any information that could be helpful. One of my neighbors gave a police report of hearing a driver speed off in the alley around 7 o'clock or so. He said that he was about to watch Billy Graham when he heard this noise, and the detectives checked and found that Billy Graham was airing around 7 P.M. The investigators had also spoken with Pierce County Transit to see what time the buses came during that same timeframe. One of the bus drivers they contacted reported that there was a car blocking the pathway for the route, which caused him to have to awkwardly make his right turn. He reported that to his dispatch and the dispatcher shared that information with the detectives.

Another neighbor had shared with detectives that she had seen two people parked in a car outside of the home for hours. She thought it was strange that the car had moved, left, then came back an hour or so later. All this talk and speculation continued to feed the local media. There was still so much speculation that the Nichols family members began to become angry with me. As we moved back into my home, the talk in the media was suggesting that this could have been my fault. That it could have been mistaken identity. I still decided to remain silent and allow Joseph to speak for me to the press.

I continued to check my voice messages. Before moving back home, I would go to the house and remove 50 messages at a time, people calling from everywhere giving their condolences. There were so many calls that I would just write them down, write the names down, the date when they called and the phone number, and just tally a list until the day we moved back into my home. My answering machine was filled again and again. The maximum capacity was 50 calls

My pastor had offered to do family counseling. He had offered to consult with the entire Nichols family, to help us start the process of healing. I didn't know if the Nichols family would accept the offer. However, I still shared with them the invitation that my pastor had extended. We started family counseling with Joseph, his mother, and Keenya's mother. Tamara was there as was I. The pastor opened the counseling session with a prayer. We had about three counseling sessions with our pastor. I was so thankful for how he was bridging some of the gaps between other family members and myself, the gap that had widened because of the media and speculation. We talked about how the investigation was going. We talked about how we could come together to get advocacy for Keenya. I was there to answer any questions that they may have had for me. We all just had no idea of who could have done this.

By May 16th, it had been about three months and counseling continued. About six months had passed and by August 16th, talks of us in the media had subsided a bit. I decided to go into a deeper clinical treatment for therapy because Tamara and I needed more support. My child began to deal with so much pain, not just hers but everyone else's. She just did not have the emotional skills to hide them. She had overheard some of the Nichols family members say that it was my fault. That if I wasn't in other people's business, Keenya would be alive. She heard so much conversation from the Nichols family that she didn't know how to protect me. Our family was always under speculation from the police, however, I was under speculation from both the police and family.

I knew then that we were in trouble. My daughter could no longer be left alone. She would no longer walk into the house by herself. She had nightmares of being shot in the face. Every night she would come into my bed and sleep beside me. I, on the other hand, could not sleep. If I went to sleep, I didn't stay asleep. I had reoccurring nightmares and pictures in my mind of Keenya's face and the bullet casing that sat beside her head. I had dreams of Keenya lying at the mortuary. I had dreams of Keenya at the funeral. I had dreams of Keenya talking to me from her grave. I had anxiety every day to the point where I experienced thoughts of suicide. I saw myself lining up a lot of Vicodin pills and taking them all at once.

ISA FARRINGTON-NICHOLS

I began the search for more defined counseling. I shared with Tamara's father that we were going to get therapy and see if he wanted to come, but he refused. He said that he didn't need any therapy. Joseph also said that his daughter, Tamara, didn't need any therapy. I begged to differ and I told him, even if she didn't need therapy, we were going to get some before she needed it. That if we weren't crazy, we were going to get therapy so that we wouldn't go crazy. I set out to find an African American, preferably female, to do our counseling and therapy. I need someone who had the same cultural values and sensitivities. I prayed that God would reveal a resource, because every time I searched for African American professionals, they did not counsel adolescents, and Tamara was only 14.

One day I talked with my *Delta Sigma Theta* sorority sister Billie Johnstone, who was also a mental health professional and had her practice. Billie had recently retired and little did I know, she was the only African American female practitioner in the Tacoma area who provided mental health therapy for adolescents. I shared with Counselor Billie the nature of what was happening to us, and she agreed to come out of retirement and to counsel Tamara for me and to be Tamara's therapist. Tamara and I both went to the sessions and we completed the questionnaire and intake information. We both were diagnosed with post-traumatic stress disorder (PTSD), major depression, and anxiety. I had not heard of post-traumatic stress disorder outside of it being something that military personnel would suffer, following combat engagement. I began to look at the research on post-traumatic stress disorder, I concluded that Tamara and I had every symptom. We fit the bill for this diagnosis. Our treatment began. Tamara was very reluctant and angry that I was insisting that she go to counseling. She had heard different comments, such as her father's, and had adopted the attitude about mental health therapy denigrating her as crazy or mentally unfit. Come to think of it, any type of mental health issue is perceived as "going crazy" oftentimes in the black community.

I had to tell Tamara that I didn't care whether she sat there with her arms folded or not. We were going to go to therapy. I explained to Tamara that she and I shared something that nobody else shared, that we saw Keenya in the devastation of the crime scene. Nobody else saw that but Tamara and myself. By the time everybody else saw Keenya, she was dressed, looking like a princess, and asleep in the casket. This was one of the main reasons why we were going to get help. I told Tamara that some people go to counseling because they are "crazy," but we were going to counseling so that we would not "go crazy." There would be help there to catch us so that we could deal with what was left of our lives. I told her that she could go by herself, or we could go together, just as long as she goes.

During the first counseling session, Tamara was not very participative. She did exactly as I thought and sat there with her arms folded. Yet Counselor Billie was well equipped to facilitate dialogue and start our counseling journey. Tamara decided that she wanted to go by herself because she thought she might want to share some things that she didn't want me to know. I said fine. We made arrangements for Tamara to go after school, twice a week. By September 16th, a month of therapy had gone by, and Tamara decided she wanted me to go with her. I agreed. Counselor Billie prescribed medication for me at first because of my anxiety. She sent me to a prescriptive therapist, who then again assessed me, and confirmed Billie's diagnosis.

We didn't put Tamara on any type of medication at that time. We felt we could control it with diet and counseling. Tamara became more volatile. And she also was very irritated most of the time. It was very hard for me to see my normal 14-year-old baby girl in this type of pain. She didn't know how to deal with her feelings, and neither did I. I felt terrible and helpless every day, so I could imagine how she was feeling. I love my child, and I was going to put all my strength into making sure she would be okay. My strength is all I had.

I had none of my immediate family here except for my stroke stricken elderly father who was in a nursing home. There was just only so much that I was going to share with him. My father is a praying man. During my childhood, he was called the "Praying Deacon." He was always a reverent praying man. My father prayed for my life during my mother's arduous and complicated pregnancy with me. Three of his previous children were stillborn births. He prayed that I would make it to term, and I did! My father's praying provided me with the security of knowing that God would hear him. That is where I needed him the most, on the threshing floor in prayer. I needed his prayers more than I would ever imagine.

Emotionally Crippled – MY REVELATION OF LONELINESS

It was October 2002. Eight months had gone by. There was no progression with Keenya's murder case. The investigation had no leads and was placed in the cold case status of unsolved murders. The hype from the media was gone. Keenya's murder was no longer breaking news. The once shocked, curious Tacoma community had resumed normal life after turning ours

RESTORE

into a circus. Few calls were coming to the house to check on our family. Today's news headlines had become tomorrow's trashcan lining.

I was emotionally crippled to the point where I could not function. I had no drive or zeal for life anymore. I was spiraling down every day. I tried to be normal. I tried to remember what normal was. The life of security, joy, and love was no longer my portion. I literally could not feel anything. I had to live for my daughters, somehow. For Tamara and Tasherra. Tamara's life was a wreck. My normal, witty, strong, and intelligent teenager was now a scared, insecure, angry, and traumatized young woman. Tamara was a freshman in high school. The transition into high school for normal teenagers is challenging enough. Now she had to transition with this major tragedy in her life.

Tamara was feeling what I was feeling but without any skills to deal with these emotional scars that we shared. We couldn't communicate well at all. We were hemorrhaging inside. Tasherra, our oldest daughter, was 19 and away attending St. Augustine's College in Raleigh, North Carolina when Keenya was murdered. Tasherra was very close with her cousin before leaving for college. They loved each other. I could depend on Keenya at times to check in with my girls to make sure that they had someone in which to confide. I don't know when Tasherra received the news about the tragedy that occurred in our home. Tasherra was independent and was strong in her faith in God. She was a praying child and now a praying young adult. I remember asking her to pray for me and to pray for her family. I could depend on her to go to the Lord. I thanked God that she was away. She was away from the rumors, the anger, and some of the resentment and animosity that was building up in some of the Nichols family.

The Nichols family had begun to shut me out of their lives. I don't know if it was intentional. They just did not want me around. My presence annoyed them, especially Keenya's mother. Joseph was the oldest son and most of his time was spent consoling his family. He was dealing with a lot of his grief. Keenya was his oldest sister's daughter. The fact that she was killed in his home practically paralyzed him. He felt that he didn't protect her. She was in our home for protection, and now she was dead. His family responsibilities were important to him. He has always felt responsible for his family. Even when I was staying with my friend, it was his role to mourn with his family. It had somehow become my role to cope alone.

The divide between Joseph and I grew wider. He was mad with me all the time. He was irritable and cold. He was gone most of the time. He and his family were going places where I was not invited. He did not tell me most of the time that he was leaving to go somewhere. He would just leave. I would receive a call from him on his cell calling to check in with our daughter Tamara. There were many times I needed to be held, but when I approached him, I didn't feel it was a good idea. I don't remember him consoling me like he consoled so many other family members. He had nothing for me. So I went through my remorse and grief by myself. I was a traumatized 42-year-old woman.

RESTORE

D.C. Sniper Shootings Linked to Tacoma – REVELATION OF BREAKTHROUGH

Many evenings I would come home and turn on the television. It was just on, out of habit, to create noise in place of my thoughts. I didn't watch it much. One evening something did catch my attention, however. There was a story about people being shot and killed somewhere on the East Coast. I glimpsed at the broadcast for a moment. I wouldn't stay tuned too long because my life was reeking with drama and trauma. The news broadcast came on again the next day. Three more people were shot and killed. The broadcast said that these were sniper shootings. Someone was randomly shooting people in Virginia, Maryland, and now Washington D.C. This was terrorizing because we were still dealing with the aftermath of the 9/11 terrorist attacks. Now a sniper was shooting innocent people in D.C.

Every day for a week there were more killings. Two women were killed in Alabama. People were being killed while pumping gas in Virginia and Maryland, even while leaving a grocery store. A child was shot near his school. A woman was killed while sitting at the bus stop. Another woman was killed loading supplies in her vehicle while leaving a *Home Depot*. A man was shot in the parking lot in front of his restaurant. He survived the bullets loaded in his chest. A taxi cab driver was killed. A city bus driver was killed while parked. The eastern part of our nation was under siege. It was apparent that we were being attacked domestically by terrorists residing in our country.

The news was full of experts and psychologists giving profiles of who this killer was. They had profiled him as being a white male. There were interviews with serial killers trying to give some indication of the mindset of this mass murderer. Some said he was a militia rebel of some sort. Nothing could describe the vulnerability that our country was going through. The East was paralyzed. The rest of the country was traumatized as we watched the latest developments.

It was Monday, October 24, 2002, when the latest development turned unusual. The trail for the D.C. Sniper was leading to the State of Washington. There were helicopters and roadblocks in a Tacoma neighborhood. The FBI and other agencies were now in Tacoma, Washington at the home of Robert Holmes. They were in his back yard sawing down a tree trunk, looking for bullet casing that could match the bullets that were pulled out of the bodies of some of the victims.

How in the heck could this be connected to Robert Holmes? Robert Holmes lived in Tacoma. I knew who he was because he served on the board of directors for the *Al Davies Boys and Girls Club*. He was the boxing coach at the club. He was respected in our community. He was John and Mildred Muhammad's good friend. Robert and John worked on car repairs together.

Now that the investigation was in Tacoma, I watched television relentlessly to find out how Robert Holmes was connected to the D.C. Sniper murders. The speculation around town was buzzing as our community waited anxiously to be apprised of the connection. The tree trunk and other fragments found in Holmes' backyard were taken to ballistics. Everything matched the same bullets from the gun that was being used in Washington, D.C. The report was that the matching bullets came from a high-powered Bushmaster Semi-Automatic Rifle, similar

RESTORE

to the military's M-16 rifle. The latest murder was that of bus driver Conrad Johnson.

How did the D.C. murders get a tip to link them to Robert Holmes in Tacoma, Washington? That was everyone's question. Robert Holmes notified the FBI that he knew who the sniper was. He called the task force and left the information. It took a few days for them to contact him back. Robert Holmes knew it was John when the media released the type of weapon that was used in the shooting. He had seen John with the Bushmaster at his home. John had built a special scope to the rifle. He had shown it to Holmes.

He recalled that John found out where Mildred was living from a private investigator that was hired for him by the Devoted Dads Organization of Tacoma. That was the organization that John used to try to get legal rights to get his children back. When they told John that Mildred was in the D.C. area, they never heard from him again. Holmes said John came to his house and told him he knew where Mildred and the children were. The last time he spoke with John he asked if he was going to harm Mildred. It was when Holmes saw the description of the rifle that he then called the D.C. Sniper task force. The investigation then went from Tacoma to Bellingham, Washington. Bellingham is located near the border of Vancouver, Canada. What a stretch. Why Bellingham?

October 26, 2002, was the day the answers to some complicated questions were answered. It was 8:30 P.M., Wednesday, and I had just arrived home from Bible study. The telephone rang at that moment, and it was my husband Joseph. He sounded frantic. He asked where we'd been and where was Tamara. I reminded him it was Wednesday night Bible study. I asked what was wrong. What was happening? He said for me to turn on the television. I turned on the television and saw the image of a man. Under his picture, the caption read, "D.C. Sniper Suspect John Allen Muhammad." I was back in a trance. My spirit inside of me was in turmoil. I had this spirit of heaviness weighing me down the whole day. I went to Bible Study one hour early to pray because I had felt a burden upon myself. It was a troubling spirit. I went to pray corporately, as well as privately for God to make known what the troubling spirit was. I needed revelation. Joseph said that he was on his way home and told me to lock the doors. I sat down and listened to the news broadcast. I numbed out emotionally and psychologically.

John was a suspect in the D.C. Sniper murders. There was also another suspect, a young boy named Lee Boyd Malvo. Looking at John's picture on the television was the eeriest feeling I ever had. John looked crazy and deranged. It was shocking that I knew the suspected mass murderer that had been terrorizing the nation, that had caused the cancelation of professional sporting events, and placed whole communities on curfew. I knew the suspected mass murderer who allegedly killed 12 innocent people and shot a young child. This was incomprehensible to me.

Joseph arrived home. We sat together and watched the latest development. There was a search for John and the boy. The FBI had given a telephone number over the television for people to call with any information that could assist them in capturing John. I asked Joseph if we should call them. He said that his mother had called the number. He said he wanted to wait until I got home. I agreed we should call. When we called, an FBI agent answered. I told them that I knew John Muhammad and that we may have some information about him. They took my name and telephone number. The agent said someone would be calling me

RESTORE

to take my information. She also said that they were receiving a lot of phone calls and it would take some time. I could imagine the many incoming phone calls. John was well known in Tacoma as the mechanic of *Express Car Truck Mechanic Service*. He worked on everyone's car at some point. He had been to many Tacoma homes doing tune-ups, oil changes, and minor repairs. Now his face was on national television as the suspect in the sniper murders.

The more we looked at John's picture the more we thought about Mildred Muhammad and the children. They lived in Maryland with her sister. The shootings were all around her. Some of the shootings were in the city that she lived in. Joseph and I discussed the possibility of John being on the East Coast looking for Mildred and their children. What other reason would he have for going there? I wondered what she was doing, looking at John's picture on the news. I wondered if she was safe. He had not been caught yet.

Was she in danger?

Was he looking for her and the children?

I tried calling her cell phone, but it wasn't on. I got on the internet to email her. I asked her to call me and let me know if she and the children were okay. After all, they had been through, now this. I asked her who was this boy that was with John. I knew it was not his son, which was the speculation from the media. John has three children by Mildred. He had two other sons from previous marriages, both of whom I had met. I did not get any response from the email I sent Mildred. She did not call me, which I thought was strange. This was something that she would have called me about. I felt something was wrong. Something had to be going on for her not to call me.

The next couple of days we finally were contacted by the FBI. Agent Marty Shane came over to the house. It was the same FBI Agent that Mildred spoke with to report her children missing almost two years ago. They told Mildred that they could not help her because there was no proof that John had left the country with them. I gave him a good hard stare. He was now at my house. He remembered me and was familiar with Mildred and my relationship with John and Mildred. I just wanted to report to the FBI what had transpired with John taking the children and them being found in Bellingham, Washington. I told him that when the children were found they were extradited to Tacoma and then returned to Mildred. I shared with him how the court had awarded her custody and granted her permission to leave the state with them. John was devastated and angry. I asked Agent Shane if he had heard from Mildred. He told me she and her children were in protective custody in Maryland. That explained the no replies to my emails.

Joseph and I shared with Agent Shane that we felt that John could have tried to kill Keenya as retaliation for my helping Mildred when her children were found and released to her custody. Agent Shane confirmed that John and Lee were in Tacoma the day Keenya was murdered. They had been arrested a couple of days before at *Market Place Grocery Store* on Pearl Street for shoplifting.

They were let go? There was just too much coincidence going on. Mildred's children were found in Bellingham, Washington. The D.C. Sniper investigation went from Tacoma to Bellingham. There was a connection to me. More connection to me than I could ever imagine.

RESTORE

The next breaking news we received was the capture of John Allen Muhammad and Lee Boyd Malvo sleeping in a rest area in Maryland. They were spotted by a truck driver who recognized the car and the description of the two and called state patrol. They were surrounded, arrested, and taken into custody. They were in an old model Chevy Caprice, to the contrary of a white van description given earlier. The car had a hole carved in the trunk of it. The back seat was removable where you could lay down and shoot through the hole in the car. The car had a laptop computer inside of it. The news showed the police removing a small tripod and a rifle from the car.

I was on my couch balled up in a fetal position watching this live nightmare consume America. I couldn't move. I felt something inside of me was being ripped apart. I knew that this was connected to me in some horrid way. My life was in the darkest season. I was in the eye of a horrible storm. The next day I received a phone call from the Tacoma Police Department stating that a man came to them with his weapons. He told the police that after seeing John Muhammad's picture on the news he needed to turn in his weapons. John and Lee had stayed with him for three weeks in February and had access to his weapons. The police stated that they sent the weapons to ballistics. The gun was a 45 caliber semi-automatic handgun. There was a match of his gun that matched the bullet found in Keenya. I asked if they were going to arrest the gun owner. The police said they had no reason to suspect him. They felt he was being honest and sincere—that he wanted to help, if possible. They had no reason or indication to think he was Keenya's killer. The police would not give me his name. They said that he had to remain anonymous because the investigation was still active.

The police said they had not tied the weapon to John, however, they were going to look for DNA. The DNA testing would take a few weeks. Keenya's mother and the rest of the Nichols' family were given the same information. Everyone was sure that he had done this to our Keenya. There was a horrible connection. I was devastated. Keenya was possibly murdered by John Muhammad. The motive was not clear at the time. My mind was running a video of events that had occurred with Mildred and the return of her three children. I was in the courtroom with Mildred the day that her children were released into her custody. Since that day many people had died. Keenya's blood had stained my floors.

CHAPTER 4

Trauma Intensified

"It may get worse before it gets better, but it will get better."
~ Mike Rawlings

The Trauma of My Drama II – REVELATION OF ABANDONMENT

The media was in sniper story frenzy. Now my house was on television again, not just locally but nationally. This time it was tied to John Allen Muhammad and Lee Boyd Malvo. It was tied to Keenya's murder. We received a call from Detective Webb from the Tacoma Police Department. He said he wanted the entire family to meet at the station. They had finished their investigation and wanted to discuss it with the family before doing a formal press conference.

My oldest sister, Sheila, was in Tacoma visiting me while all this was going on. Only God knew that I would need her on this particular day. I had been going through Keenya's tragedy alone. My family wanted me to come home. They wanted to support me and wanted me back in San Diego, California. I was their baby sister, and they were willing to do whatever to get me out of Washington. They pleaded on many occasions for me to just come home. They knew that Joseph was not there for me. They knew that his family had turned their backs on me. They knew that way before I even realized it.

Why did I stay? I rationalized in my mind that my children needed stability. The real reason was that I did not want to return home without anything. Everything I owned was in Tacoma, Washington. I did not feel that I was successful or had accomplished anything significant. I did not want to return home without having those material manifestations of my so-called successes. I would be vulnerable.

My sister and I arrived at the police station and went to the conference room to join the rest of the Nichols' family. When we arrived, we found Joseph, my daughter Tamara, and the entire Nichols family seated at the table. We spoke and greeted the others and took a seat at the table. We were waiting for the Detective to come in when DeAngelo, Keenya's boyfriend, entered. I had not seen him since he was released from jail. I heard he was coming by often to see his baby girl. Everyone greeted him, Joseph even stood and hugged him. As I stared at the warm embrace that he had received from Joseph, all I could do was wonder why Joseph had not embraced me? How could my husband embrace the man that physically abused his niece? I never received one embrace from Joseph through this whole ordeal. I tried hard to remember. I began feeling strange. I looked at each person in that room differently that day. It all became clear to me after the affectionate embrace of DeAngelo

RESTORE

that they did not care about me. They blamed me for Keenya's murder. Blood was thicker than water, and I was not their blood.

Detective Webb entered the conference room along with the police department's public relations person. He thanked everyone for coming. He said that the department was going to hold a press conference to inform the public that the bullet found in Keenya matched the gun that a man had turned in to the police. He would not say the name of the owner and only mentioned that he was cooperative. They didn't feel he had anything to do with Keenya's murder. John and Lee had stayed with this person for three weeks. John had access to this man's weapons. When John's picture appeared on the television this mystery man brought all his weapons to the police department. John Muhammad was now officially a suspect in the murder of Keenya Cook. John was in Tacoma the day that Keenya was shot. The police believed that John's motive was intended for Isa Nichols. They believed John held a vendetta against me for helping his wife regain custody of their children. The detective asked if anyone had any questions. They would answer any questions so long as they would not harm their ongoing investigation.

My sister slowly grabbed my hand. She squeezed my hand so hard that I looked at her. She wanted to get my attention. When I looked she was rolling a $10 bill in her hand. She then whispered and spoke to me saying that she was giving me energy. She was going to put the money in my hand. When I received it then I was to give it back to her. She said to concentrate on the energy. I did what she said. I was so focused on the energy I didn't hear the questions that were being asked. I just focused on the energy. I could hear voices, but I wasn't focused on whose voice it was.

I could hear comments that said, *"All I care about is Keenya."*

ISA FARRINGTON-NICHOLS

"All I care about is what happened to Keenya."
"The only thing that matters is Keenya."

I looked up at my daughter Tamara. She looked so confused. I wanted to reach across the table and cover her. Cover her ears. She heard that these two criminals came to her home to kill her mother, and now all that mattered was Keenya. The detectives apologized to the family and told us that they would be in contact with us. They wanted to ask me some questions and they would be contacting me. Everyone stood up and left the conference room. I sat for a moment processing in my mind that John had come to kill me. The bullet that killed Keenya was meant for me. We were slowly walking in the parking lot to our vehicles when I began to stand still. It felt like lead was in my shoes. I could not take another step.

My sister turned and noticed that I was standing in the middle of the parking lot. Sheila came back and stood in front of me. She grabbed my arms and began to squeeze me real tight. She squeezed me so hard that I could feel her hand touching my bone. Tears began to swell up in my eyes.

"You better not cry, not now, not in front of the Nichols!"

She said that they were not my family. I have my own family, a family that loves me, she persuaded. I was her family!

"Don't you realize, I am your family? You better not shed one tear in front of them!"

She held my hand, and we walked back to the car. When we got in the car, I didn't know where to go, so we just drove around. My sister was so angry. She was cursing and saying how dare they! How dare they say those things about you? How could they say it was only about Keenya? I was Joseph's wife, the mother of Tasherra and Tamara. They preferred you dead!

RESTORE

How could they say the things they said in front of my daughter, Tamara?

We were the breaking news story, but this time all over the world. We were on every network and in every newspaper. When I arrived home, the media was camped outside our door for blocks. My sister and I looked at the reporters. I didn't want to talk to them. We just drove by them. We couldn't go home. I decided to go back over to my good friend, Linda Braddy's house, where I stayed and took refuge some months back when the murder happened. Here I was at her doorstep again, this time with my sister. I prayed that Linda would be home. I couldn't think of anywhere else we could go.

Linda opened the door with her usual warm smile. She was chipper and warm-spirited. She invited us inside. She took one look at us at asked us what was going on. I asked her if she had watched television. She said she had seen pictures of my house on there but she thought it was the same story. I shared with her the latest developments.

My sister interrupted me and said to Linda, "My sister is in real trouble."

She began to explain to Linda the details of the meeting at the police department. Linda listened attentively as she made us some tea. She made us so comfortable. She insisted that we stay at her home for the night. We took her up on the hospitality. My sister had spoken with Linda over the phone many times in the past while I was staying with her. She was grateful that I had Linda for a friend—a friend indeed because we couldn't go back to my house for a while.

I was exhausted. I didn't have much to say. I was still devastated. My emotions were raw. I didn't feel safe. I felt so vulnerable. I just didn't know what to do with all the information. Where would I go from this point on? I felt so empty inside. The only thing I could do was pray. I wanted to pray, but I could not get any words out. I just knew that God would hear the matters in my heart. My heart was shattered, and it physically hurt. I needed Him. I needed to know that He was with me. I was surely walking through the shadows of death, and evil was present around me. I needed God to comfort me. The enemies were at my table. I needed HIS mercy, and I needed it now!

MY REVELATION JOHN CAME TO KILL ME

The next morning my sister and I went back to my house. We were able to get in without being stopped. We were inside about twenty minutes when the doorbell ranged. I could see that it was some reporters. I just let the doorbell ring. I didn't answer it. We turned on the news to see the house on the news. The media cameras had filmed my sister and me coming into the house. The media were filming the house with live coverage. The phone was ringing with reporters asking for an interview. Neighbors and friends were calling to see if there was anything I needed.

It had started all over again. I was more intense than when Keenya was murdered. This time, my home was the D.C. Snipers' first murder scene. I was the Genesis to a trail that left thirteen people dead and a nation traumatized. John was in custody at this point. I couldn't imagine what Mildred was feeling. John was so close to where she lived. I tried calling Mildred again, but I could not get any answer. I didn't know what had happened to them. A few days had gone by and I heard nothing from Mildred. I needed to talk to her. My world was now out of sync. The reality that John came to kill me was turmoil. I tried emailing her.

I wrote on Friday, October 25, 2002, at 8:30 P.M.:

...please know that you are loved very, much. please don't let anything tell you any different. GOD has a plan for you and me, you are HIS child. please don't ask why, just know that no weapon formed against you will prosper and that you will be triumphant. please know that you have blessed many, many people. please know that you are a blessing, and you are from a royal priesthood. please know that you are fearfully and wonderfully made. please know that you were given gifts, their names are Lil John, Selena, Taalibah. please know that!

PLEASE KNOW THAT FEAR STEMS FROM NO LOVE; PERFECT LOVE CASTS OUT FEAR.....PLEASE KNOW THAT GOD LOVES YOU AND SO DO I.

I'm okay.....I'm strong, and so are you....we have to be millie!!!!!

There was no reply to my emails. I wondered why Mildred had not called when she found out about John's link to Keenya's murder. I copied and pasted the first email I sent her and sent it again. I thought it was strange that she had not reached out to me and it was her husband who had killed my niece. I felt something was very wrong, I wanted her to know what I was feeling. I did not blame her for John's decision to try to kill me. Mildred and I had been through so much in the past couple of years. We had no idea that this was going to be the outcome. We had done all we could do to advise the Tacoma authorities to get John at the onset of his demented and diabolical rampage. This was just unfathomable.

ISA FARRINGTON-NICHOLS

When I did not hear from Mildred, things just ran rampant in my mind. Why wasn't she calling me? Didn't she care about what I was going through, knowing that John had tried to murder me and mistakenly killed Keenya instead? Did she not realize that I was the beginning of many other deaths, that my involvement somehow provoked her husband to rage and kill innocent people?

I woke up one Saturday morning with Mildred and her children on my mind and in my heart. I decided to try the cell phone number I had one more time. It rang and Mildred answered the phone. Mildred screamed my name at the top of her lungs. She said that the FBI had taken her and the children into protective custody. They had to leave immediately. They even took her sister and family away from the home. She said they had her home under surveillance. They were already on to John and figured out he was coming to get to her and the children. She could not make any phone calls. She didn't have access to any computer to check emails. It was so consoling to hear her voice. I felt a release of pressure now that I knew she was okay.

Mildred shared with me that she felt it could be John doing the random shooting. John's threats to destroy her would always be in her mind. He had picked up their children from school one day, took them to the airport, and boarded a plane for the island nation of Antigua, in the British West Indies of the Caribbean. They were gone for eighteen months without a trace. He would call to say that she would never see them again. He promised that she would not live to raise their children. She always looked on rooftops and around the vicinity when she was out and about town. It was only a matter of time before John would show up.

RESTORE

The shooting at the *Michaels'* store was one that Mildred often frequented. Many times she felt that the D.C. Sniper shootings were in some way meant for her and that John wanted her to know he was there.

Our conversation shifted to the media frenzy. The breaking news coverage of John's and Lee Malvo's capture intrigued us both. There were so much speculation and inconsistency. One incorrect thing was that Lee Malvo was not John's biological son. Mildred's children had shared with her that they played with Lee Malvo while in Antigua. The whole Antigua storyline I knew nothing about. I knew that once Mildred and her children got settled, they would share what went on in their lives in Antigua.

I shared with Mildred that I was invited to be on television shows. Producers from networks were calling to fly me to the East Coast to appear on their show. Connie Chung, Stone Phillips, and Larry King had left messages on my phone. Some of them had left business cards on my door. It was apparent that this story was huge. Our story was huge. John and Lee had terrorized the entire East Coast for several weeks. What were we going to do? Mildred's response was to do whatever was necessary to make some money. I laughed, but she was serious. She had a point. Sheriff Moose was already offered a book deal. He didn't know half of the things we knew. I envisioned us co-authoring our stories of love, family, and betrayal. The traumas from our dramas could encourage many abused women in our communities. Making money just didn't appeal to me though. I had chosen to stay out of the media after they took my call for help but instead fueling their sensational news stories. I didn't trust the media. The media is powerful and persuasive. When there are stories involving white victims they broadcast and avidly ask people to support them. They could raise large sums of money, depending on what they put into it. They were not interested in this little, black baby girl that was left here. From then on, I just didn't care to talk to any of them. They were like vultures, and Angeleah was their prey.

I watched television interviews with Keenya's family members. The media would capitalize on their rawest emotions. Hurt, anger, and resentment are what they captured. That hurt, anger, and resentment were targeted *at me*. The news media aired it as often as they could. They wanted to allow me to rebut, but I refused. They wanted to know why Keenya was living with me. That was a whole other twenty-one-year-old story. I didn't choose to put Keenya's mother through any more than she needed to go through. I loved her enough to just leave it alone. I wasn't going to let the media put her or myself in an emotional battle. We both were in pain. We both were in trauma.

I did not realize the sacrifice I was making to keep the media out of our personal lives. Me deciding not to say anything to the media, allowing for much speculation and erroneous communication. Everyone had a perspective of why John had killed Keenya. The most shocking for me was when one article wrote that Keenya died because of me. The *Chicago Times* reporter had interviewed Keenya's mother and took the statement and made it headlines with a full-page picture of Keenya's mother. These people that I loved for over twenty years blamed me for the death of their family member to the *Chicago Times*.

RESTORE

Abandoned – MY REVELATION OF ISOLATION

Isolation and abandonment were on every hand. I was alone. This ordeal was so huge. It was overwhelming. It became too much to share with the closest of family. It was too real. It was too scary. The only person that I could talk to was Mildred Muhammad. I could talk to her because it didn't require much. We had been through it together. We had shared this pain. Mildred was putting a life together for herself and her children. She was just as isolated as I was becoming. She was the ex-wife of a man who terrorized our nation's capital, John Muhammad, the notorious D.C. Sniper.

It was March 2003 and Mildred had responded to an email that I wrote to her. I had shared with her how bad I was feeling. I was feeling vulnerable, disappointed, and isolated. She responded to me discerning how I needed badly to talk to someone. She wrote:

Isa, I'm here. You don't have to explain to me that you need to talk. I know that honey! I am here for you as you are there for me. We have a special bond. That has been since I came to you for help with taxes. Some things we can't ignore….. for now, I'm just trying to figure out through patience and prayer, where or how I can make money for personal items, little things the children need to pay for school activities, that they want to be apart (sic) of and small bills that I have. It's difficult to try to live without money. But you know how I am. If you know my condition, why should I ask? Maybe that is the wrong way to think, but the people around me know and they don't appear as though they want to help. Kind of like it was when I was back there. So my attitude is that I made it there, I will make it here by the grace and mercy of GOD. Allah knows my heart and he will put people in place to help me. So I am leaning and depending on him and his promises. I have three examples to look at each day that his promises are true (John, Salena, and Taalibah). Have you heard anything from Dateline? You know you can contact me anytime day or night. You know that! Love Ya, Mildred.

I had heard from NBC's *Dateline*. Producers Stone Phillips and Debbie Goodison had wanted to do a story. Before them, Geraldo Rivera, Larry King, and Connie Chung producers had contacted me for an interview. I would often share with Mildred who the latest media contacts were, even though I had refused to be interviewed. I just wasn't prepared to have that level of media attention while still being in so much pain. I told *Dateline's* producers that I would give them an exclusive if they would wait to do their story. I told them that the world was not aware of everything regarding the D.C. Snipers. There was a different story that no one knew existed. The true story of the D.C. Snipers is a story of domestic abuse, domestic violence, and lack of law enforcement. It was a story of betrayal.

When I shared this particular information with Mildred she became irritated. I had not understood her apprehension. I didn't think she was serious until she became delirious with tears. She was claiming that I was betraying her trust. She had confided in me her most personal things between herself and John. Whatever I would be using to talk about or write about she did not want me to. She accused me of trying to profit from her tribulations. She even went so far as to tell me that she was going to contact her attorney to stop me.

My response to this sudden change from the woman who once encouraged me to profit in any way was accusing me of something. I didn't even understand what she was accusing me of. I had not made any commitments to anyone. I assured Mildred that I had a story of my own. My own story is one that involved my family members and me. No matter what I said, Mildred's fear and anger escalated. She threatened to sue me. At first, I reacted with the same arrogance and intensity. I told her she could sue me. I did not need her story. I had one of my own. I have a story about me and Keenya.

She didn't know Keenya Cook. Keenya Cook and Isa Nichols is a story in and of itself. That is a story of a young mother's courage and sacrifice. It is a story of domestic abuse and domestic violence. It is a story of the courage of a young mother who had to get her and her baby out of harm's way, only to meet her fate by her husband John. Why would she want to sue me for sharing my story?

I couldn't believe that after all, we had survived, we had succumbed to this. My friendship and relationship with Mildred were real. I had been on the front line with her even when she couldn't stand on her own. My friend had succumbed to fear me, that I would harm her in some way or benefit from her pain. I wrote to her on many occasions my thoughts, fears, and my deepest emotions. When her husband John and boy accomplice Lee Malvo were captured, it was evident that fate had catapulted us into areas we never could have imagined.

On September 16, 2003, I wrote what was on my mind and heart:

Mildred, I Love You and Always Will....When someone is in your life for a reason, it is usually to meet a need you have expressed outwardly. They have come to assist you through a difficulty, to provide you with guidance and support, to aid you physically, emotionally or spiritually. They may seem like a Godsend and they are. They are there for the reason you need them to be. Then, without any wrongdoing on your part or an inconvenient time, this person will say or do something to bring the relationship to an end. Sometimes they die. Sometimes they walk away. Sometimes they act up and act out and force you to take a stand.

What we must realize is that our need has been met, our desire fulfilled and our work is done. The prayer you sent up has been answered and it is now time to move on. When people come into your life for a season, it is because our turn has come to share, grow or learn. They may bring you an experience of peace or make you laugh. They may teach you something you have never done. They usually give you an unbelievable amount of joy. Believe it! It is real! But…only for a season.

Lifetime relationships teach you lifetime lessons; those things you must build upon in order to have a solid emotional foundation. Your job is to accept the lesson, love the person/people anyway; and put what you have learned to use in all other relationships and areas of your life. It is said that love is blind but friendship is clairvoyant.

Thank you for being a part of my life. May GOD hold you in the palm of HIS hand and may HIS Angels watch over you.

It was never my intention to do or say anything to betray our bond or our trust.

I explained the best way I could that I was no threat to her. I wasn't going to revisit this subject again. I let her know that I spoke with my attorney about myself and my relationships. I found an attorney that I trust. I had known him for a while. I have shared some things with my attorney, and I am going to continue. My attorney has the same code of ethics that your attorney does.

Does she talk about me with her attorney? Did she share with him who I was, or how our relationship began? It was Mildred and her attorney's advice for me to find an attorney of my own. I just didn't understand why she would think I would deliberately, knowingly betray her. I wanted her to know just how deeply I valued our friendship. I wanted to say in all sincerity:

(sic)

Mildred! You will lose me as a friend. The only way that will happen is if you walk away if you turn away.

I have shared everything with you. Everything! I told you that I would not write anything or submit anything that you did not review. I have not gone back on that. My intentions are to do what I know to do spiritually and professionally, and that is to operate ethically and in truth, and lay the most proper and efficient foundation for myself. I will use what satan intended to use to destroy me, and with GOD in the midst, directing my path, use it to save others!

You and I talked about me going out with my story first. I thought you meant that. You said you were not ready. I agreed. You said you would support me and be there. That we would be a team! That you would help me look for and expose where the explosive mines slept. I envisioned it just like back in the Phoebe House days. You trusted me then, why not now? Mildred, I still need your support and your friendship. I didn't want to be in this alone, because without you I'm alone in this thing. It has been very painful. My family living in San Diego, California is in shock and they are frightened for me. So I dare not share more than they could endure. I haven't even grieved for my niece Keenya yet.

Millie, I supported you because you needed my support. I was there whenever you needed me. When we made the vow to one another, we had no idea what the cost or sacrifice would be for me and you. We made that vow of friendship with John listening right there in our midst. Now you are out of physical danger, and you have your children back in your life. They are healthy and they love their mom. GOD is going to supply all you need, according to HIS riches and glory, according to the power that works within you. You are exhausted and I am exhausted, but GOD will re-new our strength. Our needs are different. Tamara is volatile and traumatized and blames me for helping you. My own daughter blames me for everything that is wrong in her life. She has said she hates me. I cry often because I don't want to lose the battle for her future. I'm sure you have your challenges too with teenager Lil John and the girls, if not, you will.

Mildred, you say you need money. If Sheriff Moose could get money advanced to him for only doing his job, then so can we. We know the truth! They even have Sherriff Moose dolls! If someone wants to advance me some money to share a story that has no ending in sight; then whenever I should decide to share it, then yes I'm taking it. I will send you a portion. If you don't want it, send it back. No hard feelings, no questions asked. I will not be insulted. I will put it in Trust for our children for when they become adults. Please believe that I don't care about the money. I will not be made a fool of by not getting the knowledge and instruction to protect me and us. Using wisdom as I have always done for many years professionally and in business, being slow to speak, eager to listen and then discern. I *could not say all of this until now, now that I have heard your pain. I heard your fear and concern. I do care, and I always will.*

I never really got the chance to say this to Mildred. This woman who had walked into my office ultimately walked into my life forever, a dear friend, now could not hear me in my time of need. Mildred and I could not get through it. My appeal to give her assurance failed. Somehow we shut down. We shut down seven years of trust, communication, and most importantly, friendship. We could get through all the things that came our way, but at that point, we went on silent mode. I didn't have a choice. She was the only person that could feel the depths of what I felt. Without her, I was in this nightmare drama alone. Several months went by without my friend Mildred.

CHAPTER 5

The Beginning of Justice is Near

"The arc of the universe is long, but it bends towards justice."
~ Dr. Martin Luther King, Jr.

The Trial of John Muhammad and Lee Malvo – MY REVELATION OF JUSTICE SYSTEM

The "Trial of the Century" is what the media called it, and we were only at the beginning of this new century. John Allen Muhammad and Lee Boyd Malvo's trial was scheduled to begin in the Commonwealth of Virginia. Although most of the murders were in the Maryland/Washington D.C. area, the decision had been reached to try them in Virginia. Virginia state laws deemed the death penalty for minors legal. Lee Malvo was a minor when he committed these murders, and he was going to be tried as an adult. All the jurisdictions where the murders occurred agreed that Virginia would be the place to try John Mohammad for the murder of Dean Harold Meyers and Lee Boyd Malvo for the murder of FBI analyst Linda Franklin, respectively.

RESTORE

Both trials were being tried within weeks of each other. The investigation into all of the crime scenes was going to be extensive as well as expensive. The prosecuting attorneys had a lot of information. The public defense attorney for John and Lee were the best in their field. They were attorneys with exceptional defense trial experience and strategies that won verdicts of life sentences without parole. Where would they begin to put this horrid timeline of terror into perspective? They traveled in teams around the country to many of the crime scenes, interviewing witness after witness. They interviewed victims that had survived their encounter with the deadly duo. The crime scenes and clues were collected from the state of Washington, Arizona, Alabama, and Louisiana to Washington, D.C. The timeline developed into many murder scenes that precipitated the D.C. murders.

Keenya Cook was now the focus of the prosecution team. The last murder scene connected to the D.C. sniper trail was now recognized as the first murder scene. They had finally found the Genesis of this nation's domestic terrorists. I received a call from Detective Webb informing me that the prosecution team from Washington, D.C. was in Tacoma and wanted to speak with Tamara and me. I told the Detective that I would meet with them first. I was asked to come down to the police station and when I arrived, I went up to the floor where the detective offices were located. When I arrived, it was crowded. I didn't know who was who or what was what. I felt that this thing was huge. I felt confused. My stomach was in knots. Something was wrong with this picture. I felt I needed help.

I didn't let Detective Webb know that I had arrived. My spirit was deeply troubled. I realized I had to get out of there. It didn't feel authentic, I felt like it was a set up for something. I wanted to know more about what they would require from me. I left the office and went downstairs to call my friend and practicing attorney, Gerald Burke. I could not get a signal on my cell phone so I used the public phone. I called Attorney Gerald's office and asked to speak with him. I told his secretary that I was at the police station, and I needed to speak with him. God was working that day in my favor because Gerald was in his office. I have called for him many times and seldom ever reached him on the first try. He was usually in court or a meeting with his client.

"This is Attorney Burke."

I gasped and didn't hesitate to tell him where I was.

Attorney Burke's instructions were to get up and leave. He said that I should not be talking without an attorney and that this case was too huge. He said to leave and call them back, to tell them that I would not meet with them without an attorney, to tell them that I could not afford one. Gerald had been contacted by the press when John Muhammad was first arrested. The media had found out that he had counseled John in a custody case involving his son Lynberg, who came to visit his father. John refused to send him back to his mother. There would not be any way of me knowing what their intentions were or what purpose the information I provided would serve. I left there. That was the feeling that prompted me to call Gerald in the first place. God placed that feeling inside of me when I arrived at the detective's office. Gerald was correct because this was the onset of the "Trial of the Century."

On September 15, 2003, the Circuit Court of Prince William County, Commonwealth of Virginia issued a summons for me to appear as a material and necessary witness in the Virginia trial for the murder of Dean Harold Meyers. Dean Harold Meyers was murdered in Virginia while pumping gas. My daughter Tamara who was now 16 years old was also subpoenaed. We were notified that Prince William County Commonwealth's Attorney, Paul Ebert, wanted our testimony in the event John Muhammad was convicted. we were going to testify in the sentencing phase of the trial.

I received a telephone call from Prosecutor Richard Conway. He wanted to explain to me more about our testimony. We could not testify in the penalty phase because Keenya's murder or any of the earlier murders were not material to Dean Harold Meyers' case. Attorney Conway was compassionate yet professional in our conversation. He made me feel like my experience was worth hearing. He convinced me that it would be good to allow Tamara to tell her story. The mother whose son survived his shooting while at school had the same concern for her son taking the witness stand. He shared that he testified and did well. It brought closure for him and his family. It would bring closure for Tamara. I was hesitant, but I said I would talk it over with Tamara's therapist. I wanted to make sure she could handle it emotionally. I asked Tamara if she wanted to participate. She agreed.

This would be an opportunity for me to tell my story. This gave Keenya's death significant importance. She did not deserve to die. John Muhammad should be held accountable for her death. For the first time, I felt someone cared that Keenya was slain like an animal at my front door. Up until this time, the Tacoma authorities had not advocated for our case. They just were not going to spend their resources to pursue Keenya's killer. They planned to sit back and wait for the Virginia trials to conclude. She was the first murder victim that the rest of the world knew nothing about. No description describes my relief for Keenya to be included in John's trial.

Attorney Conway explained that our testimony would only be used if they got a conviction verdict against John. After the conviction, the trial would enter a sentencing phase. The sentencing phase would allow testimony from other crime scenes. The jury has two options to consider in the penalty phase of the trial: a death sentence or life in prison. Prosecutor Conrad wanted the jurors to see the maliciousness of the suspects' actions in other shootings.

Tamara and I boarded the plane for Virginia. The Common Wealth of Virginia paid for our airfare, meals, and hotel accommodations. We were taken to their task force headquarters. We were flown in on the very day the verdict was scheduled to be read in the penalty phase. We were going to be accommodated there long enough for the jury to hear both our testimonies. If we wanted to see the trial, we could only do so after the judge would release us as witnesses.

When we checked into the hotel, I couldn't help but notice the other witnesses from Tacoma. There was a host of us that had been subpoenaed from Tacoma, Washington to come to Virginia. Most of them were police officers, forensic officers, and investigators that responded to Keenya's murder at my home. Robert Holmes, a close friend of John Muhammad, was on the list. There was one name that I did not recognize, a man that I had not seen before. He was quiet, reserved, but nervous at the same time. He looked weird. He was smoking cigarettes one after the other, always holding his head down toward the ground. His name was Earl Dancy, Jr. Who he was and why he

RESTORE

was there, would come out in the trial. He was one of the prosecution's witnesses.

Our first night at the hotel was tranquil and comfortable. The hotel had colonial-style décor. It had portraits of our history's founding fathers hanging on the walls. It made me think about my American History class in grade school. It looked and felt like Fort Knox because there were Alcohol Tobacco and Firearms (ATF) special agents everywhere. There were men and women with guns ready to use them. We were assigned our agent to escort us. I later found out that after our testimony we would have to move to another hotel. Tamara and I were going to be staying at the Holiday Inn-Isle of Capri, where family members of victims were staying.

The next morning, I awoke to the ringing of our room telephone. It was Attorney Conrad. He informed me that we had to meet with the lead prosecutor, his boss, Attorney Paul Ebert. They wanted to brief us on what we could expect during questioning. He wasn't sure exactly when we would be taken to the courthouse for testimony. Things were starting to get serious. My emotions ran so rampantly, I went numb. I couldn't feel anything. My Post Traumatic Stress was in full effect. This was going to be a defining moment in my life, and the life of my daughter, Tamara. We were going face to face with John Allen Muhammad. We were going to be within a few feet of a man that came to our home to murder me. He murdered innocent Keenya. The thing that concerned us the most was that he was going to have to face us. Would we be adequately protected? John Muhammad hated me enough to send a boy to my door to kill me. I watched too many movies when the defendant grabbed some officer's weapon and shot up the entire courtroom. Would he be remorseful? Would he be angry that I was alive and try to intimidate me as a witness? Would I snap and jump over the witness stand, jump across the table and put my hands around his deranged neck and squeeze every ounce of breath out of him?

The next morning Tamara and I woke up to prepare for the unknown. We prayed together in our room. I was still numb, and I could only imagine how my child was feeling. We got dressed and went downstairs for breakfast. We both sat there looking at the food but we had no appetite. We decided to go to the task force room in the hotel and wait for our ride to the courthouse. The ATF task force was busy, but not too busy to offer us their condolences. They were so kind and compassionate towards all of us. As for me, I had not felt this feeling before. My experience in Tacoma with our law enforcement was rigid and adversarial, to say the least. These people in Virginia were genuinely interested in me and my daughter. They took the time to include me in their work. Whatever they were working on, it was no big concealment. I asked questions regarding information that I saw on their tactical boards. They answered my questions. There was no conspiracy or secrets. For the first time since Keenya's murder investigation, I felt included. There were some answers to my questions. I saw names and locations in Tacoma that I recognized, like Mildred Muhammad and Robert Holmes. I recognized locations like Bellingham, Washington, and Tacoma, Washington.

Someone said, "Mrs. Nichols, Mrs. Isa Nichols, and Tamara Nichols."

It was time to go to the courthouse. Tamara and I were escorted to the lobby. When we arrived, several men were standing around. They were officers of the Tacoma Police

RESTORE

Department, Tacoma Fire Department, Forensics, and Coroner. There was also the timid looking black man that was smoking cigarettes, one after the other. I looked at him and smiled. I smiled because he seemed so nervous and fearful. I was nervous, but not fearful. We were escorted to different vans and surrounded by ATF personnel and undercover officers. We were heavily guarded. Every last one of them had a weapon. The ATF personnel was always courteous, but very official.

When we arrived, we were given explicit instructions to avoid the media. Media was everywhere. They could only come within a few feet as barricades were blocking them from accessing us. We were told that we had to go through security and be searched before entering the courthouse building. Our entrance to the courthouse was not the main entrance. We had to walk through long corridors and walk through many doors. I held my daughter's hand, we were both being brave. It was Tamara and I that saw Keenya's murder at our home. No one else in the Nichols' family saw that devastation. Those images will forever be in our mind's consciousness. Now, here we were together as key witnesses in the trial of the century.

Upon arriving at the courtroom we were greeted by Attorney Conrad. He asked for Tamara and me to follow him to a nearby room near the courtroom. He told us that the jury had reached a verdict in John's murder case, and we had to wait to meet Attorney Paul Ebert. There was so much activity. People were rapidly entering the courtroom. The media was pouring into the courtroom. Those of us that had just arrived had to wait in a room. Law enforcement officers were walking around with their hands on their guns in their holster. There was silence all around. We were told to be patient and be quiet.

ISA FARRINGTON-NICHOLS

It was about twenty minutes, but it seemed like an hour. Suddenly the courtroom door opened, a man ran out and shouted, *"Guilty!"*

He is guilty on all counts!

After six hours over two days, the jury had convicted him on two counts of capital murder. I moved closer so I could see. People were pouring out of the courtroom in tears. They were holding their faces in their hands. Some were walking right past me. Many were holding one another up. I could only stand there and look at the emotions of the different people walking out of the courtroom. My eyes caught the eyes of a beautiful, petite tearful Korean woman. She was crying as she was walking towards me. As I stared, my arms left my side and extended towards her. She walked right into them. I held her as she cried. She held on to me. Whoever she was, my spirit connected with hers at that very moment. I later found that she was the sister of Hong Im Ballenger of Louisiana. Hong was leaving work at a beauty supply store when she was struck in the head by a Bushmaster rifle bullet.

I could hardly walk. Never in my life could I imagine such tragedy in America. I had not felt this remorseful since the 9/11 attacks, which wasn't so long ago. I saw people coming out of the courtroom that day who somehow meant something to me. I was one of them. I was a family member of John and Lee's first murder victim. Keenya had been an unsolved murder in Tacoma. Her death was not even known to any of these hurting people. Their murders were so close to each other and so many that all the focus was on the East Coast murders. There was a murder trial that precipitated all the murders. Yet its beginning was at my front door. My life was finally on the road to some type of recovery from a time of isolation and loneliness. For eight months I had no one to share my truest feelings, fears, and frustrations. I kept so much inside. In counseling, I would talk to my therapist at The Healing Circle. The sessions were never enough time to get my feelings out. One hour was just not enough time for me. I didn't get a chance to touch the surface of my pain.

Attorney Conrad approached me and said that Attorney Ebert was ready to see me. Tamara and I followed him to a nearby room. Mr. Ebert entered and we shook hands and sat down. He said that they had just finished John's trial. We were going to begin the penalty phase, then the sentencing. Now that they had gotten a guilty verdict, the next step was to present evidence to convince the jury that John Muhammad deserved to die. The jury had only two options to consider in the penalty phase of the trial: a death sentence or life in prison. Attorney Paul Ebert was going for the death penalty. They explained to Tamara and me that we were going to be sworn in, and then asked some questions about the events of Keenya's murder. They wanted to make sure that we were going to be prepared to see pictures taken by the coroner of Keenya. The pictures would be graphic showing the bullet entry into Keenya's face. They wanted us to just tell what happened to us on that day. We needed to give details.

There were other witnesses that they were going to call that day. One of them was Mildred Muhammad. I had not seen or spoken with Mildred since our conversation on whether I should write a book about my life. I missed my friend. I did not let the attorney know that we had been estranged. Attorney Conrad seemed pleased that we would see each other again. His understanding was that we were close. He said she was arriving that evening. I asked if I could see her. He said that I could as long as we didn't discuss the case. He was going to let her know that I wanted to see her. I couldn't help but wonder if she missed me if she would want to see me.

Since the jury's verdict came, Judge Millette ordered that we start the penalty phase of the trial the next morning at 9:00 a.m. They took all the Tacoma witnesses back to the hotel. Tamara and I went to the hotel restaurant for dinner. Tamara, my baby girl, had been with me all the while. She was the reason for me to remain sane. I had to fight for us. I had made up my mind that I was not going to let her life go anywhere but upward and out of our horror. She and I had been at an emotional bottom for so long. I had to love her back to me, back to herself, back to God. I looked into her eyes sitting across the table. She was incredible. She was strong, vulnerable, and volatile at the same time. I told her that we were there to bring closure to Keenya, to seek justice for Keenya.

I received a call on my cell phone. It was Mildred. Attorney Conrad had given her my cell number. She had arrived at the hotel. I gave her my room number and we arranged to get together that evening when she checked in and got settled in her room. When we left the restaurant we ran into Mildred in the lobby. She was with a Caucasian woman. I approached them both. Mildred looked at me and smiled. We hugged. She introduced the woman to me as her attorney. I said hello and immediately focused on my friend. I asked her about the children. Before she could respond we were interrupted by her attorney. Their room was ready, and she was tired. Mildred took her room key from her. She told me that she would call me later. I didn't talk to her that evening or the next day.

At about 7:00 A.M. the telephone rang. It was the task force telling me that Tamara and I would be testifying, and we needed to be at the courthouse at 9:00 a.m. The shuttle was leaving at 8:15 a.m. It would be just a few hours before Tamara and I would be in a courtroom sitting within a few feet of John Allen Williams, now known as John Allen Muhammad. John was a black man that had turned into a coward, a sick diabolical human being. A black man that felt I cost him his marriage, his business, and his children, that I was responsible for all his problems. The price he wanted me to pay was my life. Then it became that any life would do.

When we arrived at the courthouse we were searched, given badges, and taken to the courtroom. There were the same Tacoma professionals that responded to the crime scene. There were a couple of younger white men I had not seen before. There again was the tall, skinny, dark-skinned black man smoking cigarette after cigarette. Next to the courtroom was a waiting room. Tamara and I stayed in the waiting room until it was time for us to be called to the witness stand. We heard some of the names from the people in our Tacoma group. They entered the courtroom. We were not able to hear any testimony. We could not go into the court until after we had testified and the judge dismissed us as witnesses. Once we were dismissed as witnesses we could attend the rest of the trial. I had traveled across the country. Of course, I was going to sit in John's trial. There was so much that I needed to know. The answers to my many questions were in that courtroom. It was Tacoma's time to be heard.

ISA FARRINGTON-NICHOLS

One of the sheriffs in the courtroom came up in front of where I was sitting. He said Mrs. Isa Nichols, please take the stand. I stood up and slowly followed the sheriff into the courtroom. Sheriffs were standing everywhere with their hands on their guns. John was sitting behind a table beside his attorney, facing the judge. I walked right past him. I went to the witness stand and put my hand on the Bible. I swore to tell the truth. I was asked to be seated. People were staring at me. All eyes were watching me.

I wore a fuchsia-colored two-piece suit. I wore that suit to be bright and colorful. I wanted John to remember me that day. I wanted him to see that I was still here, alive. The devil took his best shot to kill, steal, and destroy my life. I was there for John to see that Jesus saves. I took one look at John. I was breathless. I willed myself to breathe. He took a glance up at me, and I looked him in his eyes. He then looked down at a tablet and doodled. He looked so cold and distant. There was no longer any resonance of a decent husband, father, or human being. He appeared as if nothing happened. Up until I appeared there, John and Lee were just a pair of vagabonds that showed up on the East Coast. Here I was attending the trial for the murder of Dean Harold Meyers, while in another courtroom in a different county was the trial for the murder of Linda Franklin. I sat beside the Meyer family during the trial. They heard every testimony; saw every piece of evidence that the State of Virginia had to prove that John Allen Muhammad mercilessly shot their brother while he pumped gas at a local station. The Meyer family was the nicest people you could meet. They consoled me while in all their pain. They had sat in the courtroom for many months attending the trial, listening to many horrid details of how their beloved brother was brutally killed. They invited Tamara and me to have dinner with them. I knew that they wanted to know more about me. They wanted to know about Keenya. I wanted to tell them. I was now ready to share. What I had to say they needed to hear. Keenya was now included in her proper place in the chronology of victims, loved ones who were murdered.

During the week I met and dined with many family members of the victims. I sat with Denise Johnson, whose husband, Conrad Johnson, was the last victim before John and Lee were captured. Her husband was shot on his bus route. She was now a widow with two children to raise without their father. Denise Johnson's acquaintance was unique to me. Conrad's murder was last while Keenya's murder was first. I was the Alpha and she was the Omega, the beginning, and the end. Here was a beautiful sister that I had come to admire. She was gentle, yet she was strong. She missed her husband very much. She never imagined she would be living her life without him.

One evening at Holiday Inn Hotel I was invited to attend a birthday dinner for Linda Buchannan. Linda was the sister of Sunny Buchannan, who was murdered while mowing his lawn. Linda's mother had invited all of the family members of the victims to come and celebrate Linda. I managed to pick up some cheer, and so did others because when I arrived everyone was there enjoying themselves. We looked like a United Nations convention. The colors of our skin represented many cultures. These murders were random and penetrated the diversity of this country. I thought about a song I learned in the children's choir at church:

ISA FARRINGTON-NICHOLS

Jesus loves the little children, all the children of the world.
Red, yellow, black, and white; they are precious in his sight.
Jesus loves the little children of the world.

This mental video will play in my mind forever. This was an impact on my life that I would never forget.

Two years had gone by since the tragedy at my home. Family members were allowed to tell Judge Millette about our feelings. The Judge would read them before rendering the penalty for the crime. I completed an impact statement. And I wrote,

(sic)

February 16, 2004
Honorable Judge LeRoy Millette Jr. C/O
Victim Witness Assistance Program
Office of the Commonwealth's Attorney
9401 Grant Avenue
Manassas, VA 20110

RE: Impact of Defendant John Allen Muhammad's
Murder of Keenya Cook
February 16, 2002

Dear Sir;

I want to take this opportunity to thank the Commonwealth of Virginia for their support, professionalism, genuine compassion, and advocacy for Tamara Nichols and myself during the trial. We were indeed blessed to have met the many family members of victims during our stay in Virginia. We have been so isolated in Washington State, as most of the focus was on the murder crimes in the Washington D.C. and neighboring communities.

RESTORE

It was in Virginia when advocacy and understanding of my loss was finally realized. The impact stems in a horrid array of lies, deception, conspiracy, and a merciless killings (sic). Keenya's murder is no longer a mystery, or a rumor of just another black on black crime. I was a suspect along with other family members. Detectives accused me of having an affair with another man. (Talk about defamation of character!) My husband was accused of having an affair with another woman. The detectives told me that an insurance policy had been taken out on my life. (Apparently they were just probing.) My innocent, 3.68 GPA receiving daughter was accused of being connected with a gang. Until October 26, 2002 Keenya's horrifying murder was an unsolved murder. On October 26, 2002 Tacoma saw John Muhammad on their TV screens. It was at that point Keenya's killer was tied to John Muhammad and Lee Malvo; commonly know (sic) as the D.C. Snipers.

It was in Virginia when the world came to know this case as one of the worst cases of Domestic Violence in the history of this country. It was in Virginia that what was known about last to the world, was actually the first murder committed. That Tacoma Washington was the training ground for a mass murderer. That John Allen Muhammad's depravity of mind began BEFORE he lost his children in a custody hearing to his ex-wife Mildred. That he had turned his friends into accomplices that aided and abetted his warped thinking and vindictiveness.

Keenya Cook was my beautiful, intelligent, witty, resourceful 21-year-old niece. She was the youngest of three children born to my sister-in-law Pamela Nichols. Keenya was a wonderful mother to at the time, six-month-old Angeleah Rogers (Angel). Angeleah is now 2 years of age. Keenya and Angel had moved into our home with my husband Joseph (Keenya's uncle), daughter Tamara and I in October of 2001. She asked her Uncle and I if she could stay, as she no longer wanted to live with Angelo Rogers, Angel's father any longer. He had beaten Keenya on several occasions and Keenya was afraid for her and daughter Angeleah. Angelo was abusive, violent, and a drug abuser during their relationship.

Keenya, Joseph, and I sat down with Keenya and discussed some of the goals Keenya wanted for her and the baby. Joseph and I felt her goals were realistic and obtainable. Her goals were to become safe and heal from Angelo's abuse, get employment, save her money, move into an apartment with Angeleah. She had applied for the Section 8 Housing Assistance Grant, and was on their waiting list.

Every day Keenya took care of Angeleah, look for employment, look into enrolling into Vocational Schools for training. As with any extended family member, we enjoyed Keenya, appreciated her, and loved her very much.

Keenya had been in our home for three months. It was Valentine's Day; Keenya had left with the baby to go and visit with Angelo on Wednesday 2/14/03. She and Angeleah returned back home on Saturday 2/16/02 around 2:30 pm. Keenya was in a terrific mood. She had a positive weekend. She returned with a Valentine's Day balloon, a rose that she received from Angelo. Around 3:30 pm Keenya, Angeleah, and I went to the Safeway Grocery Store to shop for food. Angel was a beautiful baby girl, and we could hardly go a few feet without someone stopping to notice her. We had taken two hours, as we liked to watch Angel's expressions and reactions in the store.

Keenya and I returned home at around 5:00 pm or so. Keenya had taken the baby and placed her in a walker, while we put up the groceries. Keenya had asked if I would fix some chicken tacos for *dinner. I told her I would; however we noticed that we did not have any tortilla shells for the meal. Around 6:30 pm or so, I left to pick up my daughter Tamara from a friend's house and go back to the store. I asked Keenya to boil the chicken breast meat in some water. Tamara and I returned around 7:30 pm or so. Tamara went into the house to open the garage door for me.*

Tamara returned to the car, looking horrified. She came to tell me that Keenya was lying in the doorway, and that the house was smoky. I went to the door, and there Keenya laid. Her feet were in the doorway. Her head was near the stairway. I thought she must have succumbed to smoke inhalation. I turned off the burning pot on the stove in the kitchen. When I returned to Keenya her eyes were open and fixed, her hands were stiff and cold. There next to her head was a pool of blood. Along side (sic) of her head was a piece of metal. I jumped up to find baby Angel. The baby was upstairs asleep, lying on the bed naked. Next to Angel was a diaper, pajamas, a bottle of milk and baby lotion; Keenya had just given her a bath. I was horrified and manic. I wasn't sure if the baby was injured. When I touched her she awoke screaming and crying. I took her downstairs, handed her to Tamara, and told them to go to our neighbor's house. Tamara was stoic, she had went into shock. I had to repeat over and over to her my instructions to go to the neighbor's house. I called paramedics; they arrived and could not resuscitate Keenya. She was dead. She had been shot point blank in the face.

The impact of Keenya's murder by John and Lee is perpetual for me at this time. It was just Tamara and I that day that saw the devastation, tragic murder scene of Keenya. Tamara, who had just turned 14 years on age 2/4/2002, is now 16. She has been diagnosed with Post Traumatic Stress Disorder and Depression. Her entire life of safety, being secure and confident, and the security of living in her

ISA FARRINGTON-NICHOLS

own home no longer exist. My once normal teenager is now traumatized. Since that day she was on a downward spiraling emotion of fear, rage, and grief. She had been listening to family members share their thoughts, pain, and accusations. She began to resent me and blame me for Keenya's death. She felt that if I had not been in 'anyone else's business her cousin would be alive'. She has re-occurring nightmares of being shot in the face. She has many sleepless nights. Tamara has experimented with drugs, and almost over dosed twice. She just wanted to disassociate with the pain. Tamara is receiving therapy, and is on anti-depressant/anxiety medication. Her emotions are so volatile that her GPA went from a 3.86 down to a 2.33. I had to change her to a new school due to the notoriety of the murder. Tamara is on a Special 504 Accommodation Plan, which allows students with physical and emotional challenges special needs and support through school and even into college. I will continue to love Tamara through this, and provide what ever (sic) support that I can. GOD will heal my daughter's wounds, and scars. There is purpose and a destiny for her life.

I had no idea that John and Mildred were estranged at the time, until that day of my visit. When I stopped by to pay a visit to Mildred, John, and the children one day; I had no idea the impact would be so tragic. That it would ever lead to me or one of my family members being murdered. The impact stems from a decision that I made in the year 2000 to help Mildred Muhammad find refuge in a shelter, medical attention, and support from law enforcement for the devastation of having her three small children taken out of school, and within hours gone to Antiqua without a trace. I had no idea that John Muhammad was in the depraved mindset that he had succumbed to.

I did what any true friend would do for someone that they cared about. I cared about the Muhammad family as a whole. Today I live

RESTORE

with the impact of the loss of a beloved niece, the end of a twenty-year marriage, and a family of in-laws that I love so much, helped and provided food, shelter to walk away from me. I have re-occurring dreams of the murder scene of my home. I live with the blame for my husband's feelings of guilt for not providing the safety that he promised his niece. My husband Joseph and his family members are angry that his wife was responsible for John Muhammad's retaliation against his family.

I have to live with the pain that my decision to help Mildred caused John Muhammad to send Lee Malvo to the front door of my home with an earphone in his ear taking orders to shoot unsuspecting Keenya point blank in her face, while sixth month old Angeleah laid for hours upstairs waiting for her mamma to return. I had to live with the pain of not knowing who could do such a thing, to have no regard for another human life, while John and Lee went back to their accomplice and friend's home. Knowing how they hung around Tacoma, Washington as chameleons watching the breaking news story for weeks of the mysterious death of 21-year-old Keenya Cook. The impact of Keenya's infant daughter not growing up with her mother, now having to grow up with the assistance of the State to aid in taking care of her. I now live with impacts of economical dysfunction that are a result of my extensive treatments for major depression, sleep depravation (sic), and anxiety. Impacts that have caused financial devastation to me, while others are making profit from movies, writing books etc. as families of victims like myself have been too unstable to face the public, work at their jobs, businesses.

Keenya's murder case in Tacoma, Washington is still open. While the impact of John and Lee's trials may have brought closure to many victim murders, it brought out vital and critical information for me. Unlike the random sniper victims, Keenya's murder was pre-

meditated. The evidence is more than circumstantial in her case. John planned it as retaliation for me choosing to help Mildred find her children. It was their first mission to kill, with Mildred being their last kill. (Thank GOD they were caught within a few miles of Mildred's Maryland home.) I now live with the impact of the question of whether or not Tacoma police authorities are trying to cover-up some major mistakes that apparently occurred on their parts when Mildred was seeking assistance in the very beginning. Mildred had given several statements, reports, warning local and federal authorities of the violent and dangerous change in her husband. It was her filings of anti-harassment documents that prevented John from being able to legally purchase guns. I had provided information to Tacoma detectives on every occasion that John contacted me by telephone from Washington, Canada, and Antiqua looking for Mildred. After they were found in 2001 and the judge awarded the children to be turned over to Mildred, John never contacted me again looking for Mildred.

I offer my victim impact statement in hope that the understanding and the extent of John Allen Muhammad's, and Lee Boyd Malvo's killings deserve the recommended punishment for the crimes committed. I'm grateful to the Prince William County Commonwealth's Attorney Paul Ebert for presenting a well-structured case for the senseless and brutal murder of Dean Harold Meyers. I appreciate the integrity and professionalism extended to all family members of the many victims, including Mildred Muhammad, and her three children, for they are truly a family that is victimized. John Muhammad's depravity of mind began many years before the divorce from his wife and abduction of his three children occurred.

The inclusion of other family member victims in the Dean Harold Meyers' trial allowed for much needed support. It allowed me to look

RESTORE

John Allen Muhammad in the face and make my peace, so that true forgiveness could begin to come in and heal my hurt; thus confirming that 'no weapon formed against me shall prosper'. It fostered a very diverse group of people to come together from all over the United States to strengthen and console one another. My presence was received with much compassion and I had a chance to support others who shared similar pains. I commend the jury on their due diligence to daily sift through the horrid details, and find what was needed for them to render their decision; a decision that would bring closure and vindication to many hurting family members.

It is my hope that as Judge you will do what is necessary to ensure that John Allen Muhammad does not hurt anyone else. That as Judge you will set the precedent that the laws of our country will be adhered to, and criminals are punished to the fullest extent of the law. That as Judge you would order some level of compensation of restitution for Keenya Cook's now two year old daughter, Angeleah Rogers, and other victim families who have suffered as a result of John's crimes.

Respectfully,
Isa Nichols

CHAPTER 6

Greater is Coming

"Don't give up when dark times come. The more storms you face in life, the stronger you'll be. Hold on. Your greater is coming."
~ Germany Kent

From Pain to Purpose — MY REVELATION OF SURVIVAL

There comes a time when you have to take your pain and turn it into power. Until today I was afraid that I would never get my life back together. My daughter Tamara at this point was in her first year of college in Tennessee. My oldest daughter had finished college at Saint Augustine's College in North Carolina, married a wonderful young man, and gave birth to twin baby girls. I am the proud grandmother to twin baby girls. I saw their births. I was alive. I was alive and living. I was alive to see my family grow. I was alive to see my father look at and hold his great-grandchildren. I sold my home in Tacoma. I was living there for four years behind in my mortgage payments. For four years I was unstable and unable to work. My depression affected me physically. I owed $65,000 in mortgage payments. Yes! God took good care of me when I couldn't take care of myself.

I was waiting for my final divorce decree from my husband of twenty-two years. It was time to let go. For years I didn't have the courage. I believe God can do any and everything. God spoke to my heart. He said that my marriage covenant was made to Him in front of witnesses, not to witnesses. I kept my covenant to Him. I was His daughter. He fearfully and wonderfully created me for His purpose to do great and marvelous things on the earth. He had already prepared a table before me in the presence of my enemies. Goodness and mercy were with me all along. He was making me the head and not the tail.

God is love. His love lives inside of me. I am in a new season. Love has brought me back! I have renewed my strength and I am mounting up like an eagle. Sometimes it is a struggle, but I take every day one day at a time. I take care of myself and I am comfortable with just me. Love flows through me. I have found new roads to travel on. If I come to a block in the road I can choose to move the block or make another road. I have a lot of work to do. With God before me, I am an overcomer.

The Gift of Forgiveness — REVELATION OF GIFTINGS

I made up my mind that although my internal wounds may be deep, forgiveness heals the wounds. Forgiveness is vital to healing. I started forgiveness in two Virginia courtrooms. I looked John Allen Muhammad in his face, I prayed that Jesus Christ, son of God would have mercy on his soul. I attended the trial of Lee Boyd Malvo. I was able to see the face of the youth who was sent, to my front door by John, to kill me. He killed

Keenya as proof he could follow orders from John. I prayed that Jesus Christ, the son of God would have mercy on his soul. God had mercy for Adam and Eve after their sin. I know that the God I serve desired to heal and deliver the two that He created. He desires a relationship with them. I prayed for their families. I made my peace with them both. It was necessary for my life. Today I have a changed attitude. I have an attitude of gratitude. I am grateful to be alive. It was always that way though as I will share in the following pages.

I am intentional now about putting forgiveness in the forefront each day. I also asked to be forgiven. After Keenya's murder, I began apologizing to many people. I spent an entire year apologizing. I apologized for Keenya's death occurring in my home. I apologized for the pain that everyone had. I apologized for John and Lee not killing me. I apologized because the Nichols' family needed to hear me say it. I apologized to them at a news conference on national TV. I apologized so that people that resent me can either accept the apology or move on with their lives.

Apologies can be an impact or not. I know people that abuse their spouses and apologize shortly thereafter, or until the next abusive occurrence. If more people would apologize when they become aware of an offense, and be sincere about it, relationships would flourish. In some of the most difficult times in my marriage, receiving a simple sincere apology could have put us on the road to healing, greater love, and commitment. Some people have problems with apologizing, even when they know that they are wrong. They associated the admission of guilt as a sign of weakness in some way. I acknowledge some apologies have no sincerity. Yet I make it a point to be sincere.

RESTORE

There must be a change in my mind about how I feel about my offense, or else I won't give one.

There are areas in my life that are still in healing. Deep wounds have to heal from the inside outward. The analogy of a scab comes to mind. When I was a child, I was a tomboy. In being rough with the neighborhood guys I would encounter some accidents. I was always skinning up my knee caps. I would injure myself on my skates or bicycle too. The wound would go beyond the surface sometimes and be under the skin into my flesh. The trauma to that knee would hurt badly in the beginning. It even hurt to put medication on it to disinfect it. The next couple of days I could hardly move the leg. If I bent the knee the wound would open up and throb. I had to keep the knee still. Slowly the healing would occur. A scab would cover the opening. The scab was covering the injured area until I picked it. I picked it too soon. It began bleeding again and delayed the healing. The scab would get smaller, and eventually fall off. My sore was no longer in any danger. I could go on to my regular activities.

My emotional wounds are the same way. They are deep and must take some time to heal. Healed, delivered, and set free to minister is my ultimate goal. I have picked at the wound by sometimes going into unhealthy environments, being with people that don't genuinely care or love me. It was re-hurting the hurt. Just as it takes time to heal a deep sore, it takes time to heal deep emotional scars. You have to pamper your emotional wound. You risk letting it get infected if you don't. I don't allow any room for re-infection. I had to learn to stop picking at it or it will cause more pain. The powerful thing is that it does heal. Psalms 91 is my promise of security. In verses 14:16 GOD says:

Those who love me, I will deliver; I will protect those who know my name. When they call to me, I will answer them, I will be with them in trouble, I will rescue them and honor them. With long life, I will satisfy them, and show them my salvation.

My future is whatever God has for me. He is not finished with me. I am another epistle of a testimony. I will tell a remarkable story of God's love that transcended above hate, anger, and abandonment, into love, restoration, and reconciliation. I have more purpose to help children, families, and our communities with *InPowerMent* through transformation and renewing of their minds. As a believer in the Trinity and a survivor, I embrace the challenge.

Something of value must come from the trail of tears and shattered lives.

Jireh-Shalom Foundation is that something. *Jireh* and *Shalom* are Hebrew words meaning *provision* and *peace*. The need for provision and peace for abused women and women with children is overwhelming. Through a collaborative approach and a philosophy of unconditional acceptance, *Jireh-Shalom Foundation* offers the opportunity for truth and reconciliation to the disenfranchised; to receive forgiveness, help, hope, and guidance. The *Jireh-Shalom Model* is a transformative process that transforms domestic abuse sufferers through a process of truth and reconciliation in their lives. This transformation is a result of their self-discovery. This is my passion. This is my legacy to domestic abuse/violence survivors like myself. This may be the last thing I do for healing, education, and domestic *InPowerMent* of our children, our families, and our community.

CHAPTER 7

Truth + Reconciliation = Restoration + Redemption

"Moments of kindness and reconciliation are worth having, even if the parting has to come sooner or later."
~ Alice Munro

Restoration is an ongoing process. You do heal but you're never the same. Do you want to heal? Let go of it all. That's what I had to do. I let go of the marriage, the mortgage, the money, the enormous debt, the man of my youth, and my entire adult life. I was in bondage in a web of deception, lies, disloyalty, betrayal, and resentment. I truly felt God had left me. I was so unhappy, disenfranchised, and at times downright loco. I lost my connection to power, love, and my sound mind. I was dying. I lost the connection to love. God is love, so I couldn't feel His presence anymore. I could only imagine what Adam felt like in the Garden of Eden, walking through the garden, feeling God, and communing with God until suddenly it stops. I had fear, powerlessness, and no soundness of my mind. I was not only dying, I was not living.

Finding hope during seemingly hopeless chaos requires understanding where you were before you lost your way. When you're at the crossroads of life-changing decisions, choosing the next direction has to allow you to unlock consciousness of new thoughts and ideas. You must be willing to drop the old ways of using your mind and teaching yourself better ways to move forward. The grounds for believing something good is going to happen was not there anymore. I was so low in my life. I simply lost hope. Many days I awoke to a strong feeling of dis-ease within my soul. I somehow felt abandoned. Where did this sense of being submerged come from? Tears began to fill my eyes. My heart was beating rapidly and was being filled with sorrow. I was overcome with mixed emotions. I would lay quietly in bed to feel these emotions. Where were these emotions stemming from? What was the purpose of this now? When this sudden awakening would happen, I lay quietly, close my eyes and drift into a trance of memories.

In one memory, I saw my mother Louise Farrington lying in her bedroom, recuperating from aggressive chemotherapy and radiation from breast cancer. I was 23 years old, a brand new mom to my daughter, Tasherra, who had just finished college, and I was caring for my terminally ill mom. My mom was my foundation. She made me feel like I was a champion and could win in the game of life. She gave me the confidence I needed to not give up when I got pregnant in my senior year of college. I finished college and had my newborn seven days later. On one particular day, the imbalances of my new life were surmounting to unexplainable stress. I was in college, working, pregnant, and was not married. I was very young, and in my birth order, I am the youngest child. Perhaps it was a mix of being young and inexperienced in the realm of stress that I came home that day broken. I was trying to juggle my life in terms of having obligations and responsibilities that society was insistent upon. I was a full-time student, I had a full-time job. I was going through racial dynamics at my job, and they were treating me differently than the rest of the other employees. The 'glass ceiling' was real.

This lady, my supervisor, wanted my seat. I could sense that I was being targeted. I had been there for four years. She did whatever she could to make my life miserable. I would come in from lunchtime, she would write me up without warning, and stick it in my personnel file. She was making a particular policy for me but not the others. I was checking out on lunch when others didn't punch out, just so that she wouldn't clock me. During one particular lunch when everyone went across the street to eat, I asked if my peers had clocked out for the lunch. I was the only black woman in the department. The look of wonder and confusion began to set in on their faces. No one else was being penalized for leaving the premises during lunch. Their faces spoke volumes.

I began to start photocopying my time cards, building a case if I would be fired, and sure enough, I was. I lost my health benefits and was expecting a baby in a few weeks. I later went to the union and went to the Equal Opportunity Employee Commission. I won the case, but I was devastated and had one more quarter of school. I was hormonal, I was stressed, my world felt as if it was falling apart. That day I drove around San Jose and finally came home. I was furious and could not stop crying. My mother stood and waited for me to tell her what was wrong. She was concerned first for the baby and my health, and between breaths and the sobbing, I told her how I lost my job. My mother was 5'9, looking at her baby girl falling apart.

At that particular moment, she started stacking stuff on the kitchen counter. I'm looking at my mom, thinking, *"You're stacking stuff? What are you doing?"* She stacked them up to her forehead and waited until I stopped crying. I stopped crying in absolute curiosity. I was in wonder of what she was doing in light of my plight.

She said, *"Do I have your attention?"*

There were cups and plates and even her fine china in a single, precarious stack. The next thing I knew, she took her hand and WHACK. Everything came down crashing. The shattered pieces of what were once perfectly fine dishes. Everything was now scattered all over the floor.

She picked up the broken things, and said, *"this right here is broken, would you agree with me?"* I replied yes, and she threw it in the trash.

She held up another piece and said, *"This one is still usable. This comes from the same foundation."*

She stacked everything once again, and the things that didn't fit, she threw away. *"You have the right to push your structure over, and the things that are not working you can disregard. The things that are in good shape and are good foundational pieces, you keep. For this situation, you take out that negativity. Don't waste time on the things you can no longer use."*

I had no experience with racism before this. I was traumatized. My mom took that broken piece and threw it away. I had no idea what being a mother meant, but I had her example and this memory to guide me. So I took that piece of fine china and built it into my foundation. Some things will be broken and not reusable, some things although valuable are not reusable. You can always take what remains and rebuild. This was a life lab taught in our kitchen. I have used this memory for the last twenty-five years. Twelve months later my mother died from breast cancer. I was motherless at the age of twenty-four. I felt abandoned.

In another memory, I saw my father, James Farrington, in the hospital holding my hand telling me how much he loved me and how he didn't want to leave me. He was at the end of his earthly journey. My father was the man that protected me all of my life. He was the only man that loved me unconditionally. I was his only child that survived my mother's four miscarriages. He told me that I was one of his best accomplishments in life. He was a man that was a functioning illiterate but had a Ph.D. in life. He was a praying man and taught me how to pray, and did not send me to church. He took me to church. As a little girl, I knew how powerful God was when I saw my father on his bending knees praying reverently. He did this in our home as well as in church. At some of the darkest hours of my life, my father would send up a prayer. I admired him so much when he looked at me and showed me he was tired in his body and ready to leave. He said that Jesus had prepared a place for him. In his Father's house, there were many rooms. He spoke this three times before going into a coma. I understood how tired he was and how his depleted physical body could no longer hold his huge soul. I had no idea how I could tell him it was okay to leave me, and I was going to be okay. The truth was that I wasn't. I was terrified to be on this earth without him! My father took his last breath. Again, I felt abandoned.

ISA FARRINGTON-NICHOLS

The next memory I saw my business partner and good friend John (JJ) Eddie Jones who died in an arson fire. He was murdered two hours after I spoke with him over the phone. JJ was a long time business partner and special friend. He is the only person I knew that used language like trillion dollars almost daily. That level of dialog fascinated me. His friendship was the kind that protects and he was reliable. He always had my back. Although we were intimately close, we chose to remain emotionally close in place of sexual intimacy. JJ and I were celibate. When he died there was a hole in my heart that remains to this day. Again, I felt abandoned.

I then saw my good friend whom I had come to love as family. When her children were abducted by her husband and taken for eighteen months, I never imagined helping Mildred through it all would cost me so much of my happiness, so much of my own life. It was not my physical life but my life of love, a life of security, and a life of stability. I didn't understand the sacrifice I was choosing nor the impact of helping her. I don't have many friends, but I have a lot of acquaintances. Never before in my life had a true friend just removed themselves from me the way she had. Again, I felt abandoned.

The memory of my husband flashed before me. After 22 years of marriage the reality of my husband, no longer wanting to be married, hit me. The brokenness and disappointment I felt, all the time praying to God for the restoration of what Satan was stealing, killing, and destroying. I survived trying to pay off hundreds of thousands of dollars of debt that was based on two incomes with only my own. It was suffocating. I lost count at how many times now that I felt abandoned.

RESTORE

Relationships come and relationships go. Letting go of relationships can sometimes hurt, especially if they're toxic with abuse. My decision to stay in my abusive marriage for so long was to avoid abandonment. We don't enter relationships to end them. Someone decides to leave or stay. It takes courage to leave an abusive situation and for a long while, I lacked the courage to leave. I live with the guilt of not taking responsibility for my emotional well-being. I had been in love with one man all my entire adult life. As women, we see what we want to see. Living my own authentic life was like finding a needle in a haystack. For me to start learning how to love again, required me to go deeper within so that I could manifest it outwardly. I wanted to start loving a significant man again. I was ready to do the work in me.

I finally got to the point that I would try to become sociable again. I wanted intimacy with a partner. I longed for emotional closeness and security with a special person. I wanted someone I could be open with. I've always been open with a partner. That openness includes lessons learned from my past experiences and relationships, extending trust, believing my partner returns my feelings and devotion, and being generally comfortable with surrendering myself to him. I'm what you'd call a "hopeless romantic." I regard my partner as my best friend and foremost, a confidant. There is no hesitation I would have in discussing current problems or concerns with him. I have realistic expectations for a committed relationship. After all, I shared my life in a tell-all book. You don't get much more transparent than that. Wrong! I found out that I had no bridge to get to a partner. I had no way to cross over to love the way I use to.

ISA FARRINGTON-NICHOLS

In a recent, close budding relationship there were concerns about who I was. I shared with him a complimentary copy of my book *Genesis; The Bullet Was Meant For Me, DC Sniper Story Untold*. He said he loved me even though he had not known me very long and therefore wanted to know more about me. It was exhilarating to hear him say he wanted to be there for me and even provide for me financially. My truth is at the time, I didn't own a car. I lived with my daughter. He wanted to know why I was living this way. He felt I should be more independent. After all, everyone owns a car! Unfortunately, I believed every word that was coming from his mouth about loving me. I assumed he was a promise keeper. I soon felt like I was about to be abandoned in the new budding relationship.

I learned that abandonment has two types, willful and by circumstance. You don't control death and there are circumstances beyond anyone's control. We all are going to leave this earth. People will choose to walk out of your life. You do heal but you're never the same. How do you get the joy back that was lost when you are abandoned? For ownership of the grief to occur, the loss has to happen first. It takes time to go through this process. You have to replace the space with new knowledge, new positive experiences. Each moment God has a plan for you. Although the abandonment changes you, it does not stop you. There is comfort in knowing that God will never leave you!

I live a transparent and simple life. I remember praying to God if I could only get out of debt. I had played the game of consumerism for so long and had acquired huge debt; some of it due to the worst recession in our country. Regardless here I was being challenged with a question of how I was living. I did not feel my choices were bad decisions; however, it caused me to do

RESTORE

a self-examination. I was finally out from under the laws of debt financing. Oh, what joy I felt to be out of the enormous debt accumulated in my marriage! I share this as I felt I needed to consider the perception that I was lacking, like insufficient by his standards. The truth is my values had changed as a result of the trauma I survived. I had nothing to hide nor to be ashamed of. At a Veterans' conference, a military veteran, a woman, opened up her portion about Desert Storm with the simple sentence: I murdered people. She was not able to nurture her children, nor be the spouse for her husband. She was disconnected from it all. Trauma is trauma, not comparable, not measurable, and unique to each individual, their environment, and their ability to cope or support.

Once while watching Dr. Phil, I saw a young woman share her story. She was molested at the age of 10 through 25 by her stepfather. As she matured, he justified it by saying, he was not a biological father and that there was nothing unnatural about his advancement. She felt she had to sacrifice and endure the abuse so that her baby sister would not be touched. She didn't reveal the extent of her trauma until after she was married and had kids. What mind of a 10-year-old knows she is supposed to tell anyone? How had she reached the point where she felt she had to sacrifice?

The brainwashing had already begun, and did she have anyone to confide in? Could she even explain this in the vocabulary of a ten-year-old perhaps fearful of the reaction she imagined?

In three years John had turned Malvo into a killer. He took a young boy at 13 with a yearning and innocence to have a father in his life and became the killer. That is John's creation. His creation was spurred by massive imbalances in his life. When a person's values are negative, they become negative. Their life falls into the negative. By the time Malvo had reached his final day, he resigned himself to the negative. He was lost and dead before he even reached that chair.

We have to examine our truth. The woman on Dr. Phil started telling her truth. That war veteran began to tell her truth. This book is my attempt to tell my truth. For restoration to begin, we have to be truthful with ourselves and it takes years sometimes. It took me five years to say, *"John came to kill me."* That was my truth, my chipped cup that I put back in the pantry when I did not need to use it anymore. That was what was hurting me from ever restoring, long after finding out he did it, after the sentencing, after testifying. John Muhammad brought Lee Malvo to my door to kill me. My mom chipped her expensive China to reveal that value. That was important to her. Her set of China was something she'd accomplished and wanted to leave to her daughters. China is beautiful, fragile, and valuable. Yet she knew it could break in that structure. Some of the things we have in the structure of our lives are valuable, and even those will be thrown away when they start to hurt. You can always start over no matter what is at stake. It's a personal barometer. Some people could be toxic. Do you want them in your foundation? Some hobbies or investments may be too risky. Is that what you want in your foundation? Examine your structure and your fragile pieces of China or Tupperware and even spoons. Every aspect of life has different applications.

I was in a marriage where my husband was not coming home at night. I was checking the closet just to see if the marriage was getting by. That became my purpose as a wife, where it could have been more. I started school at the gifted age of four, and yet he constantly called me, "Dumb Ass." What was my foundation, but a crumbling and cracking plate that bore the burden of the other cracking and tumbling plates in the house? I accepted this neglect as part of my foundation. And soon enough I was neglecting myself. As a result, I was not happy, and the rest of my towering interests began to teeter and totter as my foundation turned to dust. It took years to realize that and come to that strength to admit it. I needed to create a new structure.

Activity:

What is your structure? Complete the pyramid on the following page by organizing layers of who you are and what is important to you. What do you feel is the foundational aspect of your life, and how does it relate to your other layers? Are there any layers that have to be split because two aspects of your life are equally important?

ISA FARRINGTON-NICHOLS

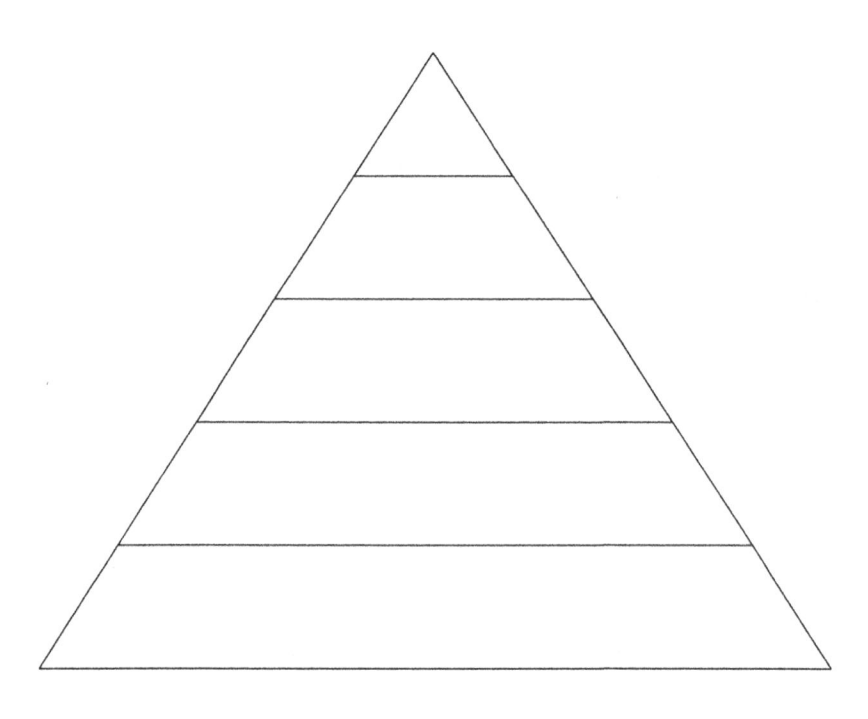

What are the most valuable aspects of your tower, and how do you measure this value?

_____
_____
_____
_____
_____
_____
_____
_____
_____
_____
_____

RESTORE

Do you feel that any layers are disjoint from one another? What sense of continuity does your structure reveal?

Which of these layers would you be willing to let go of? Which of these layers are important to expand?

CHAPTER 8

Power + Love = A Sound Mind

*"I did not give you a spirit of fear, but of
power, love, and sound mind."*
~ 2 Timothy 1:7

Love is a splendid thing. The sequence of these three attributes signifies a turning point. Within each individual is some power vested, some love, and together these contribute to a sound mind. The absence of power and love diminishes a sound mind, and in place comes fear. There are lacking components sometimes in any relationship, and make no mistake, women can be just as abusive with men as men are with women. It is not a one-way street; these three variables are conducive to a sound of mind. In the absence of power and love, people manifest their spirits of fear, and these spirits overcome them.

> *"I did not give you a spirit of fear, but of power, love, and sound mind."*
>
> 2 Timothy 1:7

RESTORE

The order of this verse is like a math equation. As an accountant, it was deposited in my spirit. I had heard this verse so many times and read it often, but the balance it presented revealed the power and unity within each individual and the care and balance we require.

Loving is a splendid thing. Learning to love the one you're with, which was me, myself, and I most of the time was not that splendid. I had isolated myself. It was during this isolation I came to the awareness to do some self-reflection. Did I consider myself when thinking about my cups? Did I consider myself when considering my needs, exclusive of any other need? Did I consider my health, my peace of mind, my sense of ease?

My husband was a good father, but as a spouse, he was not a good one. Joseph always said he would not be the same father as his father, who was known to cheat, and for the most part, he worked at not modeling his father. He refused to abandon his daughters and was there for them, but for me as a wife, not so much. The love for your spouse should be powerful, and my love for my husband was just that. I withstood many years beside him as his wife, confidant, friend, and lover. In my mind, I believed he truly loved me. As the songstress, Toni Braxton so elegantly sang *"love should have brought you home last night, you should have been with me, right by my side."* It was my greatest love, but not his.

John Muhammad lost his power, and because he disconnected, he no longer had a sound mind. Love is the key and that begins with you. John disconnected himself from God, and because of this, there was no love. His lack of power led him to succumb to abuse, and when that was not enough, he turned to threats, and ultimately he became violent and deadly. I was invited to be on a

ISA FARRINGTON-NICHOLS

Lifetime Movie | A&E Network show with Melissa Jasperson Moore, daughter of the Happy Face Killer. Melissa's father was a truck driver. He would kill women while out on the road and would draw a happy face in their blood. On the show, Melissa went around to visit her father's victims. It was her way of atonement to the family her fathered had wreaked havoc on. From there, I too started my journey of restoring love and power in my life. Soon, I started only appearing on shows with my work as an expert. I started regaining my power by requiring a moratorium from shows fixated on serial killing, and crime TV drama. The DC Snipers are a part of American History. I couldn't just keep telling everyone what happened in the past. It was time to be of a new, sound mind. It was time to share what happens after the story. It was time to show how to return to love. This was my gift to Keenya, my niece who had been brutally killed by the Sniper.

The premeditation of Keenya's murder and the random shootings that followed revealed the extent of imbalance in this man's life. Lee Malvo was floating around the island of Antigua, without love, without balance. I was in the courtroom when his parents testified. It was not uncommon, they said, for parents to go to other islands to look for work. Lee was left alone often. From that, an absence of power and the feeling of love left Malvo vulnerable. In his search for love, he lost his sound mind. John Muhammad of course sensed this void. This was Lee Malvos's test to see if he could follow orders and to win admiration in place of love. John had told him that the reason he was not with his children is because of me. The name Isa Nichols must have rung out like a sounding board and was imprinted into his mind deeply. This was Malvo's chance, and he followed orders, killing

RESTORE

Keenya when he did not find me at the home. He testified that he saw his face in Keenya's and he was killing the "old Malvo." This was only to prove to himself and the spirit that leads him there that he was worthy. Once love and power are lost, all we have left is fear. It is fearful not to have power. It is fearful not to have love. I can attest that I saw fear in Malvo's eyes when he sat there before me in court. This is some of the same fear that I'd recognized in my own eyes. Leaving that courtroom, I needed to get away from it all.

In my attempt to run away from everything and everyone at this point, I moved out of my community into one that had no public transportation service, not even a major grocery store. I left to build a new foundation and to frankly, to get myself together. It was a beautiful place. I'm not sure how I found it in the Puget Sound. I would drive on that side of town and admire the beauty that I was embedded in. I would go for long walks. It was pristine and unadulterated from the ills and lack of love of the city. I didn't notice there was not a bus line until my car broke down. That is how far away I was from my old world. We invest in images so much that we lose substance. I left the city no longer knowing who I was, for what I was living, or to what standard I would strive. I was lost. When I left to this secluded area, no one knew I was probably poor compared to them or that I didn't own my home. I didn't think I could live alone. This was a testament to that power I had in me all along, a resource I had not necessarily recognized. I always believed that I needed someone around. I thought that I had to put people around me. I had to create the type of life that I wanted to live, and only include those who I wanted to share in that environment. Those connections between people need that love, hold, and natural power within us. I had to build my confidence, that I was deserving and could love and feel love. We are all deserving of it.

I was outside of my comfort zone, away from my routines that had dressed my pain in disguise. I became empowered, whether I wanted to or not, to build a new environment. I think I was in a spiritual coma after the D.C. Sniper tragedy and the trauma of it all. After 23 years of marriage, having two babies, taking care of both terminally ill parents, running my own business for 25 years, being a good friend to my family and best friends, I realized I had given love over and above. I am good at loving others. When God said to love your neighbor, I was accomplished at it. When God said to love yea one another I was accomplished at it. When it came to loving others as I love myself I was accomplished at it. When it came to loving me I realized I was insufficient. I don't believe it was intentional. I didn't know that I didn't know. This was my first step in taking care of myself. Telling the truth about where I had abandoned myself.

Being out there in my new space, I realized that when I needed space from my marriage or my environment to find peace, I would drive in this same area. I never thought I would live out there, however, it was full circle. I was out there a whole two years. I had acquired a poodle and watched him grow to be so large, that it startled me. In a way, my dog Onyx inspired me. I had no idea what a standard poodle was, and as Onyx grew and walked around that beach, I realized, that I too could grow away from all the things that had inhibited my growth forward. I was finally in the freedom of existence that I chose and it was well within my soul. Being out in this space was some of the best times I had since the time of the tragedy. There was a winding road to get to me in a cul-de-sac. I wasn't easy to find. It was perfect for me at that time. We look to diets and exercise and hobbies to heal us, yet we overlook the thirst and yearning of the soul sometimes. My soul is most important; it was now prospering! It was truly amazing to have pure joy in my life without all the things that I had that I thought were supposed to bring me joy. I knew that any love I had now, was honest and pure. It was just packaged differently, and I still looked good. It was like a woman waking up in the morning and choosing not to wear any makeup on her face. You see the imperfection or perfection. Although you may not have a lot of money, you are still valuable. All I knew is that I was healthy and happy inside and that a new flower would be blossoming outwardly again. Even now, I'm still working with myself daily. Still learning and unlearning some things. I have habits that I watch out for. Habits whether good or bad have to be checked regularly, especially if you have gone through traumatic experiences. This new home was my pastoral retreat into considering my needs, and my ideal environment.

As a caterpillar finds its new ability to fly I am thrilled over my Spirit-empowered ability to live differently. I have good days, and I have challenging days. Trusting that I'm right where God has purposed me to be; it's what I long for. In the next few pages join me as I take God at His Word by taking the next steps to restore. Truth be told, let the truth be told!

Activity:

Consider the opening verse of this chapter. Reflect on some manifestations of love that you perceive in your life, and instances where you have encountered the opposite of love. List what comes up for you and reflect the type of impact they have on you. Do they inhibit or propel your ability to love or feel love? Keep in mind, love does not just necessarily mean a bond between you and someone else. It is a feeling of elation towards any place, thing, person, or concept.

_____
_____
_____
_____
_____

Now consider instances where you felt you had power and were in control of your situation. Were there instances where you did not have power and things became chaotic? Relate these to the extent of love that was apparent to you at the time.

_____
_____
_____
_____
_____

RESTORE

Reflect on a particular situation in your life, and examine how the following formula contributed to a positive state of mind or the lack of peace of mind.

Power + Love = A Sound Mind

CHAPTER 9

In The Beginning, God Created. Period!

"For I know the thoughts that I think toward you says the LORD, thoughts of peace and not of evil, to give you a future and a hope."
~ Jeremiah 29:11

Everyone has a divine design. Your divine design is your DNA that makes you, you. You were placed in your mother's womb at inception. You were incubated for approximately nine months, some fewer months, while others were a little more. You were at some point birthed into this world. Some were birthed alone or along with other siblings. However you made it to this realm of Earth, you were in the mind of God and born to do great things on the Earth.

I was raised with love and tender care from two wonderful parents, four brothers, and sisters. There was no trauma that I could remember growing up as a child. It was the 1960's, and I was too young to understand the days of Jim Crow or the

RESTORE

atrocities that were committed against Black people. I went to school and finished college. I met the love of my youth in college, married, and had two beautiful daughters. I raised them to the best of my ability and both and went on to graduate from college. If anyone had told me that I would have to have gone through such tragedy while physically here on this planet, I would have asked God to let me be in spirit form. I would have asked God to let me be an angel, a guardian angel. Instead, I was birthed.

It was a difficult birth, to begin with, because my mother was on bed rest for six of the nine months. She was bleeding while I was in gestation. One day my father was sitting with me, and he said there were two of us in her womb at one time and then there was only me. I had never heard this story before from my mother or anybody. I thought maybe my dad's medication was too strong when he said this, but he went on. Not to mention that there was a nurse in the room attending to my dad who explained that there were no abortion clinics or medical procedures when there were difficult pregnancies. You essentially "bled out." My twin had self-aborted. My mother previously had 4 stillborn infants before me. I survived. I was a fraternal twin with my separate amniotic sack and umbilical cord. I came to a full term at 7lbs and I was the youngest of 5 of her living children from a total of 8 pregnancies. I was born a survivor!

As we live out our lives, over time we will all have experiences to overcome. We have wants and desires in life. We desire peace, a good future, and hope. When I think back on the tragedies that manifested in my life, I simply wanted to surrender. I didn't feel like I could carry this horrific burden. My beautiful niece Keenya was brutally murdered. Her 6-month old baby girl was motherless, only to know her mother from pictures. Keenya's mother losing her youngest child, and my youngest daughter finding her cousin lying on the floor saturated with blood, left us in absolute darkness for eight months before we knew who did this horrific thing. Finding out who did it and that the bullet was meant for me, realizing my twenty-year marriage to the man I loved my entire adult life was no longer, pushed me to surrender. My friendships did not mean anything to me anymore. Friendships became extremely difficult to maintain. I learned that's when

> *"Someone is in your life for a reason. It is usually to meet a need you have expressed outwardly or inwardly. They have come to assist you through a difficulty, to provide you with guidance and support, to aid you physically, emotionally, or spiritually. They may seem like a Godsend, and they are. They are there for the reason you need them to be. Then, without any wrongdoing on your part or an inconvenient time, this person will say or do something to bring the relationship to an end. Sometimes they die. Sometimes they walk away. Sometimes they act up or out and force you to take a stand."* ~ Unknown

The friendship that I had with Mildred Muhammad, someone whose children I gave my all just to be safe, just vanished. She was gone. I believed she would be there for me as I was for her. I was there for her when her children were found after 18 months and returned to her. No one in our city believed her story of domestic abuse and that John was going to destroy her by killing her. Everyone believed John.

I didn't understand the purpose of any of this hardship. I had to ask myself what was in the mind of God. Was it to be a survivor? Was it to be a heroine? Was it to serve and/or save

RESTORE

people and be like Mary East, the founder of The *Phoebe Houses*? Was it to be humble, to persevere, to endure, and to surrender all faith to Him? I wasn't sure about the lessons I would come to learn. This tragedy was evil. Once I understood that I was created to do everything that I did, that there is an ultimate purpose that we must come to accept, it became easier to make meaning of these events. It was a divine, intertwined intervention. That's why I'm still here today. It was God's Grace that I received. It was all-sufficiency the entire time.

Activity

Take some time to think about your creation by the Creator. You were created to do great things on this earth. Identify yourself with the following.

Enter your birth name. _____

Does your name have meaning? _____

Enter your birth date. _____

What time were you born? _____

Where were you born? _____

Who are your parents? _____

How many siblings do you have? _____

What is your birth order? _____

ISA FARRINGTON-NICHOLS

Fill out the timeline on the following page. On the right side, describe in a few words the year or period in which this event occurred. On the left side explain why this event was important and if the impact was mild, significant, or extreme. Enter the year you were born just below the word *Birth*. Map the path that brought you here today, and be sure to include the positive and the hardship. A the end, enter today's date below the word *Today*:

RESTORE

Birth

Today

CHAPTER 10

Re-Membering Me – Dismemberment

"Always remember who you are. Know that you are never required to apologize to anyone for being yourself"
~ Iyanla Vanzant

A very dear friend and life coach shared with me what God spoke into her while meditating and she wanted to share it with the world. Gratefully, I was one in her world and she shared this with me. On the day that my friend died she was in her bedroom. As I walked into her room to say goodbye, she had the most peaceful look. I could feel good energy in the room. When I glanced at her room where we spent most of our time, I could not help but look at the writing she had painted on her wall with gold color lettering. It was positioned on the wall where she would see it every time she awakened and opened her eyes. In honoring her, I want to share it with you:

I AM

I am one with GOD

I am in GOD'S Love

RESTORE

I am in GOD'S Light
I am in GOD'S Protection
I am the Resurrection and the Life
I am that I am
I am who I am
I am in GOD'S Pure Clarity
I am fabulously Wealthy
I am Happy, Healthy, Wealthy, and Wise!
SO BE IT!

VALERIE ANN YARBOROUGH
10/22/2009

Often we forget how God abides within us. If we abide in Him, then He will abide in us. Many of us stop remembering ourselves because we stop, even if it is briefly, remembering God. I couldn't remember anything good and worthwhile for a long time. When we don't acknowledge this we become dismembered. Dismemberment has set in on many women and men too. The disconnection of vital social, emotional members that make us whole, can keep us broken in emotional and spiritual blockages.

We are now going to do an exercise that I learned in a Theology course I took under the leadership of Dr. Earl Fluker of Morehouse College and CEO of Vision Quest. I had to write an essay "Re-Membering My Story." It was the revelation from this exercise that showed me how emotionally dismembered I had become from who I was since my childhood. The truth was we weren't poor at all. We owned our home, and my father's employment and entrepreneurialism had provided for a family of seven. My mother had the luxury of staying at home to raise her children. I am sharing it to give an example of how you can Re-Member you.

(sic)
April 29, 2008
New Beginnings Church Conference
Spiritual Leadership in Secular Organizations:
An Exercise in Ethical Leadership
Walter Earl Fluker, Ph.D
Morehouse College

Remembering My Story
By Isa Farrington-Nichols

I remember at the age of nine going through my mother's drawer in her bedroom. I found a document that had my name on it; it read Certificate of Birth. My name is Isa Leah Farrington. I was born April 5, 1960, to James Farrington (Negro) and Louise McDaniel (Negro). I was born at 3:13 pm at Holy Cross Hospital in Birmingham, Alabama. I stared at the paper for a while when I heard the sound of footsteps coming down our hall way. Of course I put the paper back. My mother entered her room. I acted as if I was coming out of the bathroom.

It was 1969 and we were no longer living in Birmingham, Alabama. My father and mother left the state of Alabama in 1962 to move to San Diego, California. My mother finished high school. I remember my father saying that he had to get out of the South. My father completed the sixth grade in school. He could not read or write well. The only work for him was the coal mines. His father and brother both worked there. He needed more opportunities for work and heard there were jobs in California. I was the youngest of five children. I was told I was a difficult birth for my mother. My mother had several "still born" births after her fourth baby and prior to her pregnancy with me. I was told that she was in the bed for at least six months of the pregnancy.

My father was my mother's second husband. I remember learning that my last name was different than my two sisters and two brothers. They were Kelly, I was Farrington. There was (sic) fourteen years (sic) age difference between my oldest sibling and me, and eight years age difference to my sibling closest to me. I never really noticed any significant difference in us, other than I was rather red in skin coloring. My hair was blonde. As I got older people questioned my brightness. Today, we call it blended family.

Apparently, we lived in low income housing when we were in the South. I remember it being called a Project. I was told that we were poor. However, I don't remember any of it. I was two years of age when we arrived in San Diego, California. I recalled eating breakfast at dinner time. It was my favorite. My mother fixed cheese grits, biscuits, and bacon. The bacon she crumbled on top of the grits. We would pour Ber Rabbit Syrup and mash butter in it. We would sop the hot biscuit into the mixture. This food was so exquisite. One day I was reminiscing to my older sister about the food. She said we ate that way because mom didn't have enough bacon to go around. We also couldn't afford bacon slices at the grocery store. Therefore, she would buy bacon scraps from the store. She said the reason we ate breakfast at dinner time was because the food lasted longer in our stomachs. We would not have anything else to eat until the next day. If that was poor folk's food, then I'm still poor, because I still eat that way preferably

We lived in a community that was populated with mostly Blacks and Mexicans. My father worked and my mother stayed home. I remember my father saying that my mother's job was to be in the home taking care of his children. My mother was also the accountant, investor for the family. She read all the contracts, balanced all the bank accounts. She could save some money. By the time I was three my family moved to a new four bedroom house, in a cull de sac on Detroit Place. It was a new housing development. There were only black families on the entire block. I heard new words around the house like mortgage, better schools, and church.

The new neighborhood was the place that I grew up. I went to elementary school, junior high school, and high school all on the same street in the same community. All of the children on my street attended one of the schools. I remember my best friend Marcella. Marcella and I remember playing together making mud pies with water and dirt when we were only three years of age. Today we are still best friends; we remember and cherish forty five years of friendship. Marcella's family was large. They had two more than we had. They were also a military family. San Diego was known for its Navy and Marine presence. There was another family that had eight children that lived on the block as well.

Growing up in San Diego was wonderful. It was sunny all the time. We had two seasons, sun and more sun. It rarely rained. We had beautiful beaches that I would one day ditch school and go to. My life was not a life of hard knocks. I don't remember the hard times. By the time I was thirteen I was the only child left in the household. All of my siblings were grown. Two had gone away to college, and one had gone into the workforce. I don't know how my oldest brother missed the Vietnam draft. But he did. Of course we had the "black sheep" sibling. I remember real drama in there with my mom saying that there will not be two grown women in her house! Our house shut down at a certain time at night. If you were out passed that time, you were not going to get inside unless our parents let you in.

My father had started businesses. He was always finding ways to make some extra money. That was how he was able to buy whatever he wanted. We had new cars, we went on family vacations. I remember

RESTORE

him starting a janitorial business. When he got his first commercial building the whole entire family had to help. It was a doctor's office. My job was to empty the waste baskets, and then put an empty bag in the waste basket. There was a wastebasket at every desk on two floors. One evening before leaving the building my father beckoned "Isa Leah". When I here (sic) my entire name, something is wrong. I responded yes, daddy. I went flying down the hallway to where the voice came from. Standing over a waste basket was my dad. I looked in the waste basket and there was a yellow Juicy Fruit Chewing Gum rapper (sic). Oh, my GOD! My daddy started yelling, my mother and everyone came to see what the commotion was about. There I was about to get my tail tore up over a chewing gum rapper (sic). Thank GOD for my mother's intervention. She managed to convince and remind my father that I was just a child, and he should explain what is wrong. Daddy talked so long until I would have preferred the whipping. It would have been a lot shorter. The moral of the story was that the gum rapper (sic) could have cost him the contract. It could have been the difference between him getting the contract and the next guy. He said if I am cleaning toilets, I should get recognized for the cleanest toilet. To this day I don't chew Juicy Fruit Chewing Gum, and I perform my best effort at whatever I do.

I remember when I was in high school I played sports. Track and Field were my talents. I was fairly independent. At sixteen I got my first job. I was so active that I wasn't home much. The more active I was, the less my mother and father were around. I was the last child, and I had plans to go away to college. My parents were doing things separately, which was different for them. They were growing apart. My mother had sent my father back to school to get more education. His learning to read allowed him to become confident in himself. He was no longer at a loss for words. He could hold a conversation with anyone. His self-esteem and pride were at an all time high. He wore suits and sport jackets and slacks. My mother had his teeth fixed at the dentist. He smiled a lot more. He began to join social clubs. My father became an Elk, Mason, and eventually my mother became an Eastern Star. Socializing for them went on almost every weekend.

I remember the day my whole life changed. One day I came home from school and there was a note on my bed. It was from my mother to me. She was letting me know that she had left my father. She said that she wanted me to stay with my father and she would come back for me. She told me that she needed me to be strong, continue to go to school. She said she needed some time to herself. She said she was depressed. My heart was beating so fast, I thought it was going to bust. I read the letter over and over again. I wondered what I was going to do without my mother. I had no idea that she was even unhappy. I just didn't notice her depression. I waited for my father to come home from work. When he arrived, I was scared to come out of my room. He called for me to come to the living room. When I got there he was sitting on the couch with a letter from my mother in his hands. I sat beside him and he told me what I already knew. My mother had left. He said he didn't know why she left. My father's face was sad. He said that everything was going to be alright. I didn't show my father the letter that my mother wrote me. I had to believe what she said, and that was she was coming back for me.

Two weeks went bye (sic) when I found out that my mother had went to my oldest brother's house to stay. She was there the whole time. My mother returned back to the home. She wanted to get my father's attention; she wanted him to notice that she was hurting. My father was going out and not including her. She said that he was seeing one of my friend's mother. My father denied it. My dad wasn't seeing the woman my mother accused him of, but he was seeing one. My mother's intuition was correct. Eventually my parents divorced. My parents were well respected. My father was a respected man, a deacon in the *church. The entire community was shocked. They were perceived to be the happiest, stable couple that had everything.*

In 1978 I graduated from Morse High School. I was accepted at several colleges and universities. Their divorce was economically devastating. There was no money for college. I received several scholarships. I accepted the offer from San Jose State University. While in college I pledged Delta Sigma Theta Sorority. I fell in love with my college sweet heart, eventually the father of my two children. In 1983 I graduated and received dual degrees in Radio/TV Broadcasting and African-American Studies. I minored in Business Administration. I supported myself in college as an accountant. It was there I built a career as a public accountant. Today I have a public accounting practice for twenty years. I am a consultant, community service leader in my community. I am an ordained Minister of five years. My two daughters are adults. I have a wonderful son-in-law and three beautiful granddaughters.

Activity:

Now you will write your own essay entitled "Re-Membering Me." In the space below develop an outline, then write about yourself. You have an opportunity here to write about your best self. Write a few paragraphs in this workbook and then you can expand on it later. This is to help you get it all out on paper, to revisit, and to make sense of the events you listed in your timeline. Think about the world you live in today. You have been living in it for a certain amount of years. You have heard that you are this and you are that, but do you truly know who you are in this world? Think about all the experiences you've had: some good, bad, and downright ugly. There are impressions left from experiences that mold us in some way. Take some time and write who you think you are.

Consider the world we are in today versus the world in which you were born. What has changed between then and now? What has remained consistent throughout the years, and what has disappeared entirely? What sustained these aspects that remain, and what drove out aspects? Truly think deeply upon these questions, beyond the culture that may have changed. What meanings changed in your life? What people? Try to reach an understanding as to who you are today based on these thematic changes to your narrative. Be honest about your condition.

After you are done, revisit your essay after a week or so. Approach it with a fresh mind. What are the physical aspects of how you see yourself? These are important because they are the easiest for us to see, whereas our internalized damage will become visible with added due diligence. If you ever want to measure how you are doing at any given time physically look around you. Are the bills paid? Are the bills not paid? Any shutoff notices? Are there clothes on your back and in your closet? Do you have a car? Is there gas in your car?

Is this the manifestation of you that you want to be? If not, what would you change if you could? You were not put here to be able to pay bills or not pay bills and then die. God's thoughts of you are *"to give you a future and a hope."*

RESTORE

Name: _____

Date: _____

Essay Title: _____

ISA FARRINGTON-NICHOLS

CHAPTER 11

The Truth Is:
A Personal Life Reconciliation Statement

*"There is a time for everything, and a season
for every activity under heaven."*
~ Ecclesiastes 3:1

Truth-telling is a delicate space. A lot depends on what truth is for you. Whatever is true about you is something that you have to accept. There has to be some ownership of it. A lot of discontentment in life has to do with one not owning the truth. It may sound obscure here for a brief minute because owning the truth is not as easy as we would like to believe.

I was chosen by God and selected by DeVos to participate in this program because I demonstrated the potential for effective ministry leadership in the Tacoma Community. The program is grounded in the belief that by investing in leaders like me, people who have already demonstrated leadership skills, our youth in our communities will benefit. This was ideally just for me, as I was stuck in a rut. The resources for the Academy and for Jireh-Shalom Foundation, where I had worked for almost ten years, were stretched too thin, nearing a breaking point. I was volunteering most of the time as the funding diminished from the worst recession in America. It had hit the philanthropic industry hard. I was being stretched too thin and nearing a breaking point as well. I was so pre-occupied with 'doing,' believing that there was value in my "busy-ness." The two most important features of the DeVos Urban Leadership Initiative are the Core Values and the Breakthrough Skills. The two elements worked together and I was indeed on life support professionally and personally. I needed an Intensive Care Unit and DeVos was it.

Getting to the truth is challenging and I was able to get there, in some part, because of the guidance these core values presented. Even though the truth really can bring about freedom, it can be a hard pill to swallow. It's easier to be in denial. It's easier to live a lie. I found myself living a lie. I believed what I was doing in my personal life was the right thing to do. Spiritually, I thought I was doing the right thing. I believed the stacking order of putting my family, church, career before me was the right thing to do. When the truth is I am first after God, and that I am an umbrella to those that are dependent upon me. If I was not healthy then those who needed me would receive an unhealthy me.

The revelation of this truth came as I was opening up a bank statement. Yes, a bank statement! When is the last time you reconciled a bank statement? Many of us do not take time to do this every month or we don't feel the need to reconcile. We either trust the bank's accounting or we say we can do the math in our head. A bank statement is a tool the bank sends you to reconcile your account on deposits with them. It shows every transaction for the month, beginning with your beginning balance, which is where you started. The next thing it shows is your deposits, which is what you have put in it on a particular day. The next thing it shows is withdrawals that you made, and other deductions from your account on a particular. At the end of the period, you are either positive or negative. If there is a discrepancy you would be able to detect it because your balance should be correct. On the back of the statement, there is a ledger that allows you to list every transaction that came in and out of the account. It is a line by line of the truth. If you had a negative balance, then you withdrew more than what was available to you. If you had a positive balance you deposited more than you withdrew. This is the state you want to be in.

The truth for many is an imbalance. Your life is imbalanced and you need to reconcile. Often we continually go around not recognizing when we have not replenished ourselves. We withdraw time after time. Our personal life gets depleted before we have deposited sufficiency. We often end up insufficient. Insufficiencies cause you to be in lack. When we are lacking in your emotional wellbeing, lacking in your physical wellbeing, lacking in your spiritual wellbeing is so easy to succumb to lack and shift ourselves out of balance. You must always take a self-examination to make sure you have enough deposits going into yourself to cover all the withdrawals that you expend to live your best life. Your life needs replenishing. One cannot go on day to day just giving everything away. You have to just stop expending talent, energy, and your peace all the time. Every time something comes along and we have to withdraw from our reserves to cover a request from someone or something, we do it without thinking anything about it. Everybody needs something from you, whether it's a spouse, child, elderly parents, etc. These withdrawals from you can render you bankrupt if you're not careful. Your life has balance when it encompasses all the things you want in it. Oftentimes we know what we do not want. Well, that half of the battle, and a good place to begin bringing balance into your life. Replenishing your emotional, physical, spiritual well-being will create abundance. Talent and your gifts will create energy for renewal. Energy and renewal will give you peace.

Did I replenish myself? Heck no! That's why I'm writing it now. I was in an airplane traveling from Washington State to Washington, D.C. I was watching the Steward prepare me for take-off. I love to fly. Even when they disappear or crash, I'll still ride on an airplane. I'll catch an airplane to go across the street. You get the picture. Watching the Steward say the things that I've heard many times before about how to fasten and put on my seat belt, where I should go to find the emergency exits, really important information that I pay attention to. When he began to talk about the oxygen, and how it worked if we needed it in case the plane lost cabin pressure, I had a revelation that shocked me. This man told me that the oxygen mask was going to come down. He told me to put the oxygen mask over my mouth first. Then put the oxygen mask on others next to assist. For the first time, I understood what I was doing wrong in my approach to being restored. My life looked like this.

RESTORE

Life Balance Sheet

Deposits	Withdrawals
Rest	Insomnia
Nutrition	Poor nutrition, fast food, processed food
Exercise	Working 10 hour days
	Ministry
	Sorority-Community Service
	Depression
	Anxiety
	Family
	Friends

During the entire trauma in my life, I was not putting the oxygen that was necessary for me to breathe on first. I had not stabilized myself so that I could assist others. I was making sure everyone had the oxygen first, and then I would put on my mine. The revelation was so powerful my eyes rolled back in my head and I went to sleep. I was knocked out. By the time I woke up, we were already in Washington, D.C.!

ISA FARRINGTON-NICHOLS

Activity:

Now that you have examined the transitions in your life, their implications, and your need to maintain a balanced life, use this table to measure what you are withdrawing from your life and how you are replenishing. By examining the dates, try to determine a pattern. This will help you determine if you need more replenishment, when, and how.

My Life Balance Sheet

Date	Deposits	Withdrawals

CHAPTER 12

Establish Your Purpose with Value

"He who has a why to live can bear almost any how."
~ Nietzsche

The purpose of creating a life balance sheet is to derive value. If things are in the negative, then the value is naturally negative. Value in this sense is those aspects of life from which we derive a *positive balance.* Now that you have listed your withdrawals and your deposits, we must understand how the transactions of life can bring you more meaning, and ultimately, a clear and defined purpose.

As I mentioned earlier, I participated in the DeVos Urban Leadership Initiative and was introduced to a set of core values. It was a result of this coursework that I was able to reconcile my life of imbalance back to balance. The DeVos Urban Leadership Initiative is a venture of the DeVos families. The DeVos' were the founders of AMWAY (a billion-dollar company) that believed in high values of faith, family, and stewardship. This initiative was developed in response to a challenge from parents Richard and

Helen DeVos to their children and their children's families to work together on a family philanthropic project. The families began to work through a process in 1995 to determine what values and common interests would guide the development of the vital project. The process resulted in a national faith-based leadership initiative that ultimately seeks to make a positive impact on the lives of disadvantaged, urban youth, and the communities in which they live. It's labor-intensive work; you have to have a passion to be in this field of work as it is heartbreaking sometimes.

The five core values are:

- Accountability
- Balance
- Interdependence
- Empowerment
- Leverage

Accountability. Knowing the importance of personal integrity by regularly seeking feedback and guidance from trusted sources. The program encouraged me to know myself more fully by examining my call to ministry. I also had to be accountable through caring and supportive relationships with other participants.

Balance. Jesus taught his followers the importance of caring for the whole person – spiritually, physically, intellectually, emotionally, and socially – and took time to do that for himself. During the program, I had to examine how I spend my personal and professional time. I saw that the way I spent my time matched up with the things that were most important to me. I learned that there was a healthy tension between competing priorities.

Interdependence. The church is the community of God's people, a community with a divine purpose, abundant gifts, and a place for everyone to belong and to serve. I learned the importance of working 'in community," collaborating effectively, and relying on relationships with others to achieve a common goal.

Empowerment. In the early church, the calling and discipline of new leaders contributed to its rapid growth and the spread of the Gospel. I learned to identify and develop leadership skills in those around me.

Leverage. God builds His Kingdom by transforming our hearts as well as our circumstances, with many people participating through a great many closely interwoven actions and effects. The core value of leverage stresses the importance of looking for ways in which seemingly small actions can have a powerful and lasting impact on the Kingdom. There is a time for everything and a season (Ecclesiastes 3:1).

Activity:

What do these five values mean for you? Once you have an idea in your mind, find a piece of scripture, a quote you like, a movie, book, or individual that exemplifies the meaning of these five values. This will help expand the idea in your head and define the value by making it relevant to you and who you are. Then create two actions that you can commit to daily and overtime to ensure you are keeping these values as an active part of your life.

1. Accountability:

Daily Action:
Long Term Action:

2. Balance

Daily Action:
Long Term Action:

3. Interdependence

Daily Action:
Long Term Action:

4. Empowerment

Daily Action:
Long Term Action:

5. Leverage:

Daily Action:
Long Term Action:

CHAPTER 13

EXODUS – *It's time to move on!*

And God said to Moses, "I AM WHO I AM."
~ Exodus 3:14

Understand that God is! His name is "I AM WHO I AM." Rest on this foundation. Your mind, will, and emotion depend on this understanding. Many times in my life I have been stuck and scared. I was stuck to where I was in a rut of dysfunction, scared to where I was at the point of immobility and no movement. I had no motivation to do anything. I felt like my life had no purpose. I was functioning, but not functioning. It was so difficult to move. I was paralyzed emotionally as I was completely drained from investing my emotions where they could not be contained to grow. I was paralyzed physically as I did not exercise or go out anywhere and only exposed myself to the thoughts of trauma. I was uninvolved. I was paralyzed spiritually as I stopped spending time praying, meditating, or worshipping corporately.

It is at this moment that you'll know it's time to move. Movement can be a difficult process. I felt I was paralyzed.

Moving involved much work. The whole process was an overwhelming consciousness for me. Yet there will come a time in life that we have to move to get our life back on track! Many people enter mental institutions with the hope to be healed from the debilitation of their trauma. In the black community, less than 5% of the population receive treatment for mental health issues. I had to get my 14-year-old daughter, the one who found her precious cousin murdered on our floor, and myself into counseling so that we would not go crazy.

We have to move onward and forward. The destination is to deliverance. Deliverance from any type of bondage. I was in bondage to my memory of the tragedy that took the life of an innocent person. I felt that I failed to protect my loved ones. I felt that somehow I could have done something differently, and could have had a different outcome. Whether it's oppression, depression, or suppression, deliverance is from wherever you are and into your best life. What we must realize is that our need has been met, our desire fulfilled and their work is done. The prayer you sent up has been answered, and it is now time to move on! When people come into your life for a season, it is because your turn has come to share, grow, or learn. They may bring you an experience of peace or make you laugh. They may teach you something you have never done. They usually give you an unbelievable amount of joy. When my niece moved in with her baby girl I loved helping her care and nurture this beautiful new life. I loved the smell of the baby powder in the fold of her little neck. I enjoyed watching a new mother balance her new role as a new mom.

Believe it! It is real! Lifetime relationships teach us life lessons. They teach us those things we must build upon and motivate us

RESTORE

to keep moving forward. Your job is to accept the lesson, love the person or people in their own, unique ways, and put what you have learned in all other relationships and areas of your life. Receive God as "The Lord who heals you." Healing is His nature. His Will is to make us whole. Preparation is the first step. Rely upon God. He is the Lord, your banner. As you surrender to Him, your victory, miracle, and protection will be all you need to succeed.

> *And Moses built an altar and called its name. "The LORD IS MY BANNER…." Exodus 17:14*

Stay alert to seek out God's work. It will often come in a way we do not expect. Be careful of complacency. Complacency usually settles in and it creates habits. Not all habits are good, and not all habits are bad. Habits are an acquired mode of behavior that has become nearly or completely involuntary. Our experiences will affect the habits that we form from the experiences. I experienced ridicule from people that felt I should not have helped my friend Mildred in her domestic abusive situation. As a result, I developed a habit of justifying what and when to be there for someone. I was struggling with self-confidence in making those kinds of decisions. Stay alert to the reality that you may have to form habits that will affect your relationships. There is safety in His arms. You will be upheld on your new journey. That's who Jehovah Jireh, God the Provider is! Once He reveals the idea or the opportunity to do what it takes to move forward, ask God to be a lamp unto your feet, and light unto your path. Then move! You want the skills and abilities to take your first steps from your dramatization.

Activity:

Below write a scripture, poem, or something that you can affirm and will motivate you to move. It can be as simple as Get up! Get dressed! Get out! It can be "I can do all things through Christ Jesus who strengthens m." The intention is to create a resource that you can come back and read daily to help strengthen you on your journey.

_____
_____
_____
_____
_____
_____
_____
_____
_____
_____
_____
_____
_____
_____

CHAPTER 14

RESTORED – *The Life You Deserve Now*

"...then the man prays to God, and he accepts him; he sees his face with a shout of joy and he restores to man his righteousness."
~ Job 33:26

God is aware of your situations and your circumstances. I was able to trust in Him to help me. Some of us have to trust in Him again, as we have lost our way. We have to come to know the superpower of God is in control. He will bring you back to where you were before you lost your way. I had to clear my mind of all negativity and past disappointments. Let darkness go, and set your mind on light and life. Life is worth living again. This is a choice and it will take discipline. The more you direct your thoughts, the more doors will open for good things. Zeal and joy will become yours to know again.

Take some time to deliberately think about things that bring hope and encouragement. Finding hope during seemingly hopeless chaos requires understanding where you were before you lost your way. When you're at the crossroads of life-changing decisions, choosing the next direction has to allow you to unlock consciousness of new thoughts and ideas, dropping the old ways of using your mind, and teaching yourself better ways to move forward. For some, the grounds for believing something good is going to happen is not there anymore. I was so low in my life I simply lost hope until one day I raised my hand, raised my chest, raised my head, and let it go. There is a song that I listen to where the lyrics say *"I want a heart that forgives because a heart that forgives is freedom."* Let it go! There is no future in the past! Wisdom is made from experiences and for every trial I learned the lessons. You don't have to settle for the status quo. You can recreate yourself. Just give yourself time to do it and restore yourself.

> *"Trauma is not just an event that took place sometime in the past; It is also the imprint left by that experience on mind, brain, and body. This imprint has ongoing consequences for how the human organism manages to survive in the present."* ~ Dr. Bessel Vam Der Kolk

Heartbreaks and hurts don't heal fast. You have to allow the pain to be felt. I had to learn that pain does not mean that I'm weak. This is the understanding that is the foundation for the journey out of trauma and into the life you deserve right now. Trust the wisdom that created you! Raise your hand, raise your chest, and raise your head. There is no future in the past. It's like looking in the rearview mirror while driving forward. Always look out the windshield. It's much bigger and you can see it further. Your destination is restoration. We do not have to live in the bondage of a web of deception, lies, disloyalty, betrayal, resentment.

RESTORE

Often I would get extreme anxiety and panic attacks from thinking about things, persons, circumstances from the past. Just recently I reached back and re-connected with Mildred, the friend whose life held up a mirror to my own life. I had not spoken with or seen her in 13 years. I was looking back at how great we were before we became estranged. For some reason, I felt we could somehow pick up where we left off. I missed the friendship and the support we gave to one another. So I invited her to speak at a conference. I was excited that I was in a place to pay her speaking fee, travel, room, and board. On the day of the event, 70 mph winds were knocking out power throughout several communities, trees had fallen on the major freeways. This impacted the 150 will-call ticket attendance of the conference, and I wasn't able to pay the expenses including the speaker fees. I was blamed for the extreme weather that caused 85,000 homes to be without power. I started to feel those feelings of rejection and abandonment creep up again.

Thirteen years had gone by without any reconciliation of our lives that had intertwined for four years before the 18 months of her children's abduction. When the children were found and reunited with their mother, I thought I would continue to be a part of their lives. I was looking for closure of some sort. I had memories of the close friendship we had. I gave her whatever she needed of me to survive the abduction of her children. I would pray with her. I had other Christian organizations praying for her and the return of her children. The Phoebe House provided food and shelter. The YWCA provided legal services and resources. I utilized every resource and connection I had to aid her in staying alive, and hopeful. I would give her what money I had. Aside from the mosque and her husband, Mildred had few friends.

None of them seem to be around. Many of them she thought would help her did not. Mildred could call me any time. I believed she was my friend. Then I realized when I needed her to be there for me to talk to and open up to about things in my life, she was not there like I longed for her to be. After John murdered my niece, I could not even talk to her. She had not reached out to me. The last attempt to find my friend was in Washington DC. I contacted her and she agreed to join me. I was a keynote speaker at a luncheon and had purchased a ticket for her lunch. There I was with an empty chair beside me. Mildred did not show up. Mildred was nowhere to be found. I felt abandoned and rejected yet again.

I should have let that old friendship stay right where it was…. behind me! Instead, I re-injured myself emotionally. We were similar people at one time but in 13 years we were not the same. Wisdom was made from that experience. I learned not to be reactive and to continue to be confident. There is a saying "a setback can lead to a comeback." It takes courage and grace. We all deserve comebacks.

Finding hope during seemingly hopeless chaos requires an understanding of where you were before you lost your way. When you're at the crossroads of life, changing decisions and choosing the next direction allows you to unlock consciousness of new thoughts, and ideas. It teaches us better ways to move forward. I like to call it *Brilliancy Mindset*. Brilliancy Mindset focuses on your spirit ruling over your body. It's a necessary hunger for spiritual, emotional, and physical change. It is a mental spark. You can be transformed to have the life you deserve now by the renewing of your mind. The life you deserve now is in direct alignment with what God has created for your rewards in life. Your focus has to be on intimacy with God. This can be a challenge as it requires communication with God through meditation and prayer. I have come to find that many have *prayer scaring* when you prayed for something and you didn't receive what you prayed for. Remember some things only God knows when we're ready to receive them. He has an appointed time and season for you. Your ways are not His ways, and your timing is not His timing. Keep communicating with God until your victory is won. You will have the life you deserve, and you will have it more abundantly.

Brilliancy Mindset focuses on dreaming again. I didn't know how I was going to make it back from such detrimental traumas, but the images in my desire to have a life deserving of truth, reconciliation, forgiveness, happiness, and unspeakable joy became real to me. My mind opened up to the future—to the possibilities of new opportunities, new relationships, and new beginnings. The life you deserve is your promise land. It will take as long as it takes. Just don't give up. There were so many times that I became discouraged. After the sensationalism of the DC Snipers diminished, I felt no one cared what I and other family members of John Muhammad and Lee Boyd Malvo's victims had to do to get our lives back. What were we going to do to stop this from happening again? Who was going to stand and use their voices to talk about weapons of mass destruction, such as a Bushmaster assault rifle in a civilized society, or domestic violence? You may be the one to have to be transparent with your story or "TEST-imony" to save someone else from your fate. I was on a journey; I knew what I had to do to get the life I deserved restored.

Restoration is your destination now. Trust your intuition that there is something powerful within you. This will free you to focus and practice "re-membering" yourself. Go from a break down to a breakthrough into the life you deserve now. Go through the process, whatever it is, whatever you have to do. Achieve the extraordinary! Restoration and redemption are yours.

Often in the night, a poem would arise in my anguish, and I would scramble out of bed and begin to scribble my thoughts. The thoughts that arise from sleep when the body is resting have always been mysterious and yet purposefully planted. This poem came to me in one of those instances where I truly believe God was telling me, it was time to restore.

RESTORE

As given to me by the HOLY SPIRIT
April 25, 2015

I NEED THEE, OH HOW I NEED THEE

LIKE A SPHINX ARISING OUT OF THE ASHES – RESTORE

LIKE THE BROKENNESS THAT SHATTERS OUR HEARTS AND MINDS – RESTORE

LIKE THE GUILT AND SHAME THAT PLAGUED ME DAY AFTER DAY – RESTORE

LIKE THE ANGER THAT WAS SEVEN LAYERS AROUND MY WOUNDED HEART – RESTORE

LIKE THE BITTERNESS THAT WAS MY TONGUE – RESTORE

LIKE THE COVENANT RELATIONSHIP THAT BECAME UNDONE – RESTORE

LIKE THE IMPURITY I ALLOWED TO PENETRATE MY ESSENCE – RESTORE

LIKE THE MISPLACED WORDS OF DEVOTION, HE PROMISED IN MY PRESENCE – RESTORE

ISA FARRINGTON-NICHOLS

LIKE THE FRIENDSHIP PROMISE THAT WAS ABANDONED – RESTORE

LIKE THE FILLING OF A HOLE FROM A CANNON – RESTORE

LIKE FROM THE INSIDE OUT – RESTORE

LIKE FROM THE BOTTOM UP TO THE TOP – RESTORE

LIKE THE LOVE YOU SHOWED ON THE CROSS – RESTORE

LIKE THE LESSON ONLY YOU GOD COULD HAVE TAUGHT – RESTORE

LIKE THE NEW JOY THAT ONLY YOU COULD HAVE BROUGHT – RESTORE

LIKE ME, THE ONE THAT FORGOT THAT ONLY YOU GOD, FORGOT ME NOT – RESTORE

About Isa Farrington-Nichols

Isa Farrington Nichols is a National Speaker on trauma reconciliation and a critically acclaimed published author of *Genesis: The Bullet Was Meant For Me: DC Sniper Story Untold*, and her latest work, ***RESTORE: Truth and Reconciliation Through Traumatic Experiences.*** She is the CEO of Jireh-Shalom Foundation/Maxine Mimms Academies non-profit organizations.

Isa is a popular guest on TV shows including Larry King Live, Fox and Friends, OWN, DISCOVERY CHANNELS, BET, VICE TV, AND Lifetime/A&E delivering heartfelt revelation and insight to the traumatization of her family when her niece took a bullet meant for her from this country's most notorious murderers called the DC Snipers. Trauma traumatizes whether it is from rape, incest, war or seeing Michael Brown lying on the street of your community in Ferguson, Missouri for hours. In her second book RESTORE Isa Farrington Nichols has done her part with her "love in action" journey to restore her life back from pain and sorrow. RESTORE is her recovery and victory in life as she begins to love herself truly. With great courage and compassion Isa leads in truth telling in such a way that the most ordinary of us can understand that human dignity and grace can be restored, even after a time of unexplainable, unacceptable pain. Isa is the proud mother of daughters Tasherra Farrington-Nichols, and Tamara Farrington-Nichols along with four granddaughters, twins Aleera and Tameera, Akeera, Terrah.

Made in the USA
Columbia, SC
13 July 2022